Anticipating and Managing Crime, Crisis and Violence in our Schools

Anticipating and Managing Crime, Crisis and Violence in our Schools

A Practical Guide

Jo Campbell

CAMBRIA
PRESS

Youngstown, New York

This book has been registered with the Library of Congress.
Campbell, Jo
Anticipating and Managing Crime, Crisis and Violence in our Schools / Jo Campbell
p.   cm.
ISBN-10: 1-934043-37-0
ISBN-13: 978-1-934043-37-0

*To all who have suffered
because of school violence*

Table of Contents

Appendix A
Sample Crisis Manual 71

Appendix B
Federal Communications 101

Appendix C
Suggested Sources for Further Information 119

Acknowledgments

I gratefully acknowledge all those educators, colleagues and friends who have shared their stories with me over the years and who have had the courage to open up after dealing with the excruciating pain of dealing with school crisis. After talking personally with people from Jonesboro, Arkansas and Jefferson County, Colorado, I was so impressed with their fortitude through their turmoil. They are great role models and true American heroes.

Very important in the formulation of this book are all the educators with whom I have worked all these years. Through the myriad of safety and security issues, both large and small, I have learned a great deal. May you all continue to be as dedicated to a secure learning environment.

Anticipating and Managing Crime, Crisis and Violence in our Schools

Introduction

During my first years as a teacher, a local law enforcement officer at a school meeting suggested that everyone involved in a particular highly volatile child custody case carry a gun and learn to watch for bombs under their cars. The immensely serious issue of safety in schools became very clear to me, then a novice educator.

Over the years, there have been numerous incidents in the world of education that merit grave concern. A few come to my mind—taking loaded guns away from students, dealing with threatening parents and students, reacting to strange gas smells and smoke in the school, bomb threats, and staff members with questionable intent. In the face of such issues, the first-year administrator soon realizes that no university class taken in administration prepared them to handle such issues.

Although there are many resources on crisis intervention—much more now since 9/11—most of these focus on only one aspect of planning. Administrators often learn to deal with crisis situations as they are happening, with very little support from others or any guides to help them make crucial decisions in a moment's notice.

The purpose of this book is to provide a guide to help prepare for various possible crises in schools. It shows how to train staff so that they can react in a purposeful and effective manner during various types of crisis situations. It also illustrates how to take care of all involved after a crisis and how to ensure proper documentation of the crisis. This is an important guide in today's environment of escalating safety uncertainty in schools.

It first became very apparent to me that the horror of school terror can occur anywhere when Cokeville Elementary School in Wyoming was the target of a May 16, 1986, domestic terrorist attack. David Young, a deranged former policeman, and his wife took over the school with a cache of weapons and a large bomb transported on a cart.

When Angels Intervene to Save the Children, a book that was based on that incident, was later made into the NBC movie "To Save the Children," it brought national attention to the fact that such a situation is not limited to large urban districts. This incident personally cemented the need to have crisis plans in schools, no matter where they are located.

One of the most important and frustrating aspects of public education is the growing issue of safety in schools. It is a tremendous responsibility for those in school administrative positions to protect the well-being of our youth.

How many people remember diving under their desks to supposedly be safer in case of nuclear war? Practice and drilling is not new. In the history of public schools, emphasis was placed on such drills to escape schools in the event of fire, or to seek protection in case of tornados and hurricanes.

However, today's safety issues span a much broader spectrum. In addition to fires and natural disasters, schools must now contend with safety issues that range from school shootings and abductions, to bombs, bio-terrorism and hazardous materials.

School administrators have a myriad of challenging responsibilities, such as the No Child Left Behind annual yearly progress goals, ethical assessment practices, hiring and mentoring quality staff, managing marginal staff, meeting growing needs with decreasing budgets, increasing costs, business pressures on educational responsibilities to keep America competitive in an increasing global economy, sex offenders and child abuse registries, and the changing demographics and demands of the school populations.

Safety and security is of prime concern, but many administrators have little time to give it the full attention it deserves. This book was written to be part of the solution to this problem. This book is a guide that will create awareness of various possible crisis situations, and appropriate security plans and procedures. It is important to note that there are no cookie cutter plans that districts can reproduce. To have effective crisis procedures, it takes work from every individual school in the district to deal with the uniqueness of that particular site.

In Chapter One, the status of the public school crisis is reviewed. The recent history of school safety and security concerns is shared. The most recent developments in school safety are discussed along with a look at what may be in store for administrators in the future. Specific strategies are also offered in the identification of potentially violent individuals.

Chapter Two details how one school district went from fully open doors in all buildings to an award-winning district for safety and security. Included in this chapter are specifics on how to conduct a facilities audit with local authorities as well as a step-by-step process on how to create a district crisis manual. Support resources are offered in Appendix A.

Chapter Three focuses on crisis prevention. District requirements for practice and drilling are shared. Risk factor analysis and the principle of triage are discussed, along with suggestions for staff preparations with incident stress. Information on how teams respond to crisis and work with the community in creating incident commands is also included in this chapter.

Chapter Four delves into the communication with and the involvement of community and district stakeholders in the preparation of a crisis situation. An example of a simple practice drill and a local community drill is offered in this chapter.

Chapter Five includes possible sample crisis scenarios. Actual step-by-step explanations of what might happen are provided. Reflection on what went well and what might be improved upon are listed for consideration.

Chapter Six concentrates on strategies a school district might use to help all those involved in violence and crime start down the road to recovery. Suggestions on what to do once the "all clear" announcement is made to actually going home after a crisis are shared.

In Chapter Seven, suggestions on what a district could do to learn from the crisis are offered. Specific guidelines are shared for group debriefing, beginning a counseling program with those that require further support, and ensuring that no individual affected by the tragedy is left out.

Chapter Eight poses a series of review questions that are meant to be a mental checklist for preparedness. These questions help us consider crucial details in a comprehensive safety and security plan.

Appendix A furnishes support resources in the creation of actual crisis manual writing. Many manuals are printed with one page per plan, so that if a particular crisis occurs in a building, the specific page can be torn from the manual and used as a checklist. It is suggested that any plan be studied to be National Incident Management System, so it is NIMS compliant. The templates offered are only examples that a school district can use to begin creation or review their own—they are not meant to be copied since each school plan must be specific to the school district.

In Appendix B, a copy of the Department of Education warning on school preparedness is provided.

Appendix C includes further resources that might be pursued.

Chapter One

School Crises—
Past, Present, and Future

In this chapter, discussion and exploration will focus on:

- The increasing importance of safety and safety concerns for school administrators
- A comparison of past security and safety plans in comparison to what is needed today
- Indicators of possible violent students
- Case File Risk Factor Analysis Form for possible violent students
- How violence escalates
- What to look for in potentially violent persons
- Terrorist attacks on schools
- A timeline of some worldwide school crisis situations
- A general procedure to follow during any crisis
- Handling of hazardous materials and germ warfare
- Why terrorists target schools
- Steps in handling bio-terrorism
- Steps in handling a bomb threat
- Procedure for the aftermath of a crisis
- Documentation
- Communication and Other Crises

The Increasing Importance of Safety and Safety Concerns for School Administrators

The horror of school violence in recent years causes great anxiety to all responsible for school safety, reinforcing the need for optimum preparation as far as possible. At times, these preparations can be so overwhelming that there seems no obvious place to start. This chapter gives an overview on how we can begin to make our school districts safer for staff and students.

Schools have a legal obligation to provide a safe environment for their staff and students. According to the authors of *School Crime and Violence: Victim's Rights*, schools are charged with the responsibility to provide a harmonious environment for learning. They are charged with the care, custody and control of behavior of all people while in that environment. All those in schools have a right to be protected against suspected criminal actions, criminal or violent activity which can be prevented by normal supervision, and identifiable people who are dangerous, including staff, students and community members who are allowed into the building.

In addition to fulfilling their legal obligation, ensuring safety also helps serve the purpose of schools—education. It goes without saying that a safe environment promotes both learning and teaching. Providing such a safe school environment is a challenge since threats can range from discipline issues to bio-terrorism. A school safety plan is like a huge puzzle with parts that are constantly changing. Once a plan is in place, other concerns will crop up that will call for a revision of the original plan.

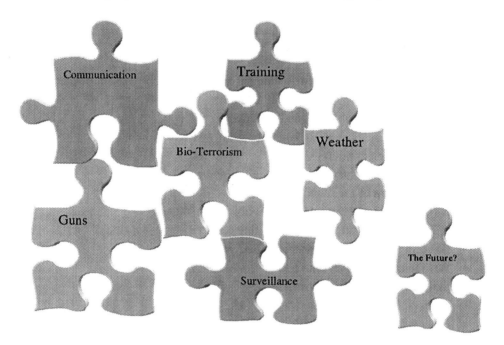

The multi-faceted issue of school safety involves all kinds of aspects, including facilities, programs, staff preparedness, communication plans, and so on. These concerns have changed drastically over the years and will continue to evolve. School districts in the past have had plans in place, such as evacuation plans and hazardous material handling.

A Comparison of Past and Present Security and Safety Plans

In the 1980s, plans often resembled the following:

School District Safety Plan
Evacuation Plan
Fire Control
First Aid
Accident Investigation

In the1990s, plans were revised to include additional concerns:

School District Safety Plan
> Evacuation Plans
> Fire Control
> First Aid
> Accident Investigation
> Bus Safety
> Bomb Threats
> Blood Pathogen Issues
> Reporting to Authorities
> Documentation
> Tornado/Hurricane Plans
> Hazardous Materials

These plans need to continue to grow and evolve with developing issues:

School District Safety Plan
> Evacuation Plan
> Fire Control
> First Aid
> Accident Investigation
> Bus Safety
> Hazardous Materials Handling
> Blood Pathogen Issues
> Reporting to Authorities
> Documentation
> Tornado/Hurricane Plans
> Bomb Threats
> Hostage Situation
> Bio-Terrorism
> Drug Induced, Uncontrollable People
> Sex and Child Abusers
> Suicide in and out of School
> Acts of War
> Acts of Domestic Terrorism
> Gunfire / Workplace Violence
> Flash Floods
> Earthquakes
> Hazardous Material Spills
> Winter Storms / Heat Concerns
> Deaths on Premise, etc.

Indicators of Possible Violent Students

Recent statistics indicate that a quarter of all our students and staff have been a victim of a violent act. Nationally, one student in eight has carried a gun to school. Boys are also more likely to be a victim of school violence. Why are there increasing cases of school violence? The FBI reports that most shooters who are white males between the ages of 8 and 18 reported that they did it because they felt bullied and picked on in school.

Police say that there are four common factors:
1. Lack of parental supervision at home
2. Lack of parental involvement at school
3. Student peer group pressure
4. Involvement in drugs and alcohol

There has been a great deal of research on what to look for in students that may be predisposed to violence. The potential violent student shows multiple signs such as below:
- Displays cruelty to animals
- Uncontrollable angry outbursts
- Repeated truancy, suspension or expulsion from school
- Lack of supervision and support from parents or a caring adult
- Reading materials dealing with violent themes, rituals and abuse
- Habitually makes violent threats when angry
- Name calling, curses or uses abusive language
- Previously brought a weapon to school
- Serious disciplinary problems
- Few or no close friends
- Drug, alcohol or other substance abuse or dependency
- Preoccupied with weapons, explosives or other incendiary devices
- Victim or witness of neglect or abuse in the home
- Been bullied and/or bullies and intimidates peers or younger children
- Tends to blame others for difficulties and problems they cause
- Prefers TV shows, reading materials, movies or music expressing violent themes, rituals and abuse
- Depicts anger, frustration and the dark side of life in school writing projects
- Member of a gang or an antisocial group on the fringe of peer acceptance
- Depressed and has significant mood swings
- Threatened or attempted suicide

The following is a chart that a school district could use to determine the likelihood of students becoming violent. Using student ID's across the top instead of names protects the privacy of students when sharing aggregate reports with committee members working together to determine whether the school has troubled students capable of violence.

Case File Risk Factor Analysis Form for Possible Violent Students

Risk Factors	Place one of the following indicators for each risk factor (each youth) √ = Confirmed, S = Suspected, N = None, Unk = Unknown										
	ID #	ID #	ID #	ID #	ID #	ID #	ID #	ID #	ID #	ID #	ID #
Individual											
Aggressive/Disruptive behavior											
Hyperactivity/Impulsiveness											
Pregnancy and delivery complications											
Parental abandonment											
Depression (youth)											
Substance abuse, including alcohol (youth)											
Drug dealing											
Delinquency referral before age 12											
Positive attitude towards antisocial behavior											
Prior out of home placements											
Social isolation											
Victimization - Neglect											
Victimization – Physical abuse											
Victimization – Sexual abuse											
Unemployment (if not attending school)											
Family											
Young mother											
Maternal depression											
Criminal behavior – Caregivers											
Criminal behavior – Siblings											
Poor parent-child communication											
Poor parental supervision											
Poverty/low socioeconomic status											
Serious marital discord											
Harsh and/or erratic discipline practices											
Family violence											
Substance abuse, including alcohol - Caregivers											
Peer Relations											
Delinquent peers											
Gang membership/involvement											
Peer rejection											
Bullied by peers											

School													
Learning disabilities													
Poor academic achievement													
School suspensions/expulsions													
Disciplinary referrals													
Elementary school behavior referrals													
Negative attitude towards school													
Truancy													
School dropout													
Community													
Economically depressed neighborhood (youth's)													
High crime neighborhood (youth's)													
Drug activity													

Office of Juvenile Justice and Delinquency Prevention (OJJDP)

How Violence Escalates

The following is a graphic on how violence increases over the years:

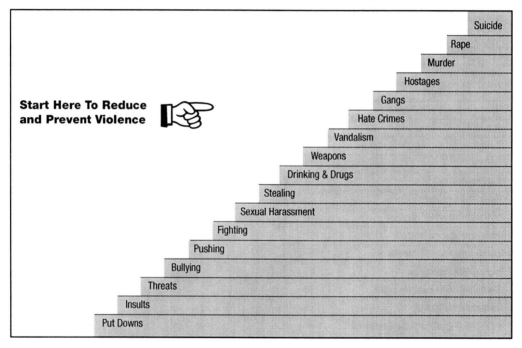

The Violence Continuum

The Montana Behavioral Consortium states that the Violence Continuum is an awareness tool developed by the Billings Care Campaign and utilized by the MBI to create awareness that violence begins with behavior and attitudes that each individual has the power to control. People think of violence in terms of the criminal behavior that makes headlines, but violence does not begin with abuse or brutality. It begins with a selfish lack of concern for others. The Violence Continuum is not intended to encompass all violent acts or to suggest a rigid order of offensiveness. It is a general indicator of the escalation of violent behavior.

To prevent violence, community and school involvement in proactive efforts must be added to existing effort.

What to Look for in Potentially Violent Persons:
- Grades or work begin to fall off.
- Change in friends.
- Spends a lot of time alone.
- Cruelty to animals.
- Sudden change in dress.
- Access to large amounts of cash.
- Shortened temper and sudden outbursts of anger.
- Fascination with weapons.
- Threats of violence to self or others.
- Persistent disregard for or refusal to follow rules.
- Involvement in gangs or suspicious people.
- History of bullying.
- Expression of violence in drawings or writings.
- Involved with violent media.

When working with any person, whether it is a student, staff member, friend or family member, there are general guidelines on how to respond to the people that exhibit behavior described as above.
- Work with others in a caring and supportive manner.
- If a co-worker or student you encounter shows signs of possible violent behavior, share this information with your supervisor, and possibly, the police.
- Report immediately any warning signs such as writing on walls or notes found. It is important to act by making a formal report.
- Never assume they are just having a bad day. Always err on the side of caution. Too much is at stake.

Terrorist Attacks on Schools

An area of concern that has recently been considered as a possible issue for schools is terrorism. Although a terrorist attack upon a school in the United States may be improbable and unlikely, the first step toward preparedness is admitting that it is at least possible that terrorists could strike a school or schools in our country. Even the U.S. Department of Education, a federal agency characterized for years by their denying and downplaying of the potential for a terror attack upon American schools, issued an advisory to schools in October of 2004 with recommendations for heightening security and emergency preparedness in light of the 2004 school attack in Beslan, Russia. (A copy of the letter can be found in Addendum B in this book.)

There seems to be conflicting beliefs about terrorism and schools. On one hand, some consultants, speakers and trainers appear overly alarmed by the issue of terrorism and schools, while on the other hand, many public officials, consultants, and trainers take the politically correct position of downplaying or completely dismissing the possibility of a terror attack on schools since doing so is consistent with the wishes of the bureaucracies with which they are associated. This, however, does not mean the possibility does not exist. The Secret Service states that there is increased "chatter" on the likelihood of a terrorist attack on schools.

School Shootings

The prevailing sentiment on school shooting is, "Oh, but it will not happen here or those incidents always happen in urban schools districts, not in sleepy little towns." It does happen in all types of schools, by all types of people, and all over the world, not just here in the United States. Increasing school crisis situations involving shootings have been reported and the following list is a sample of these horrific situations:

A Time Line of Recent Worldwide School Shootings

May 16, 1986 Cokeville, WY	Man and woman held a group of teachers and students. Their bomb exploded, killing the woman and burning some of the hostages. The man committed suicide.
May 21, 1988 Winnetka, MN	A woman walked into a classroom and killed an 8-year-old boy and wounded six others.
Sept. 26, 1988 Greenwood, SC	A 19-year-old opened fire at Oakland Elementary School, killing two 8-year-old girls and wounding nine other people.
Jan. 5, 1989 Little Rock, AK	A 16-year-old student was fatally shot in the playground.
Feb. 2, 1996 Moses Lake, Wash.	Two students and one teacher killed, one other wounded when 14-year-old Barry Loukaitis opened fire on his algebra class.
March 13, 1996 Dunblane, Scotland	16 children and one teacher killed at Dunblane Primary School by Thomas Hamilton, who then killed himself. 10 others wounded in attack.
Feb. 19, 1997 Bethel, Alaska	Principal and one student killed, two others wounded by Evan Ramsey, 16.
March 1997 Sanaa, Yemen	Eight people (six students and two others) at two schools killed by Mohammad Ahman al-Naziri.
Oct. 1, 1997 Pearl, Miss.	Two students killed and seven wounded by Luke Woodham, 16, who was also accused of killing his mother. He and his friends were said to be outcasts who worshiped Satan.
Dec. 1, 1997 West Paducah, Ky.	Three students killed, five wounded by Michael Carneal, 14, as they participated in a prayer circle at Heath High School.
Dec. 15, 1997 Stamps, Ark.	Two students wounded. Colt Todd, 14, was hiding in the woods when he shot the students as they stood in the parking lot.
March 24, 1998 Jonesboro, Ark.	Four students and one teacher killed, ten others wounded outside as Westside Middle School emptied during a false fire alarm. Mitchell Johnson, 13, and Andrew Golden, 11, shot at their classmates and teachers from the woods.
April 24, 1998 Edinboro, Pa.	One teacher, John Gillette, killed, two students wounded at a dance at James W. Parker Middle School. Andrew Wurst, 14, was charged.

May 19, 1998 Fayetteville, Tenn.	One student killed in the parking lot at Lincoln County High School three days before he was to graduate. The victim was dating the ex-girlfriend of his killer, 18-year-old honor student Jacob Davis.
May 21, 1998 Springfield, Ore.	Two students killed, 22 others wounded in the cafeteria at Thurston High School by 15-year-old Kip Kinkel. Kinkel had been arrested and released a day earlier for bringing a gun to school. His parents were later found dead at home.
June 15, 1998 Richmond, Va.	One teacher and one guidance counselor wounded by a 14-year-old boy in the school hallway.
April 20, 1999 Littleton, Colo.	14 students (including killers) and one teacher killed, 23 others wounded at Columbine High School in the nation's deadliest school shooting. Eric Harris, 18, and Dylan Klebold, 17, had plotted for a year to kill at least 500 and blow up their school. At the end of their hour-long rampage, they turned their guns on themselves.
April 28, 1999 Taber, Alberta, Canada	One student killed, one wounded at W. R. Myers High School in first fatal high school shooting in Canada in 20 years. The suspect, a 14-year-old boy, had dropped out of school after he was severely ostracized by his classmates.
May 20, 1999 Conyers, Ga.	Six students injured at Heritage High School by Thomas Solomon, 15, who was reportedly depressed after breaking up with his girlfriend.
Nov. 19, 1999 Deming, N.M.	Victor Cordova Jr., 12, shot and killed Araceli Tena, 13, in the lobby of Deming Middle School.
Dec. 6, 1999 Fort Gibson, Okla.	Four students wounded as Seth Trickey, 13, opened fire with a 9mm semiautomatic handgun at Fort Gibson Middle School.
Dec. 7, 1999 Veghel, Netherlands	One teacher and three students wounded by a 17-year-old student.
Feb. 29, 2000 Mount Morris Township, Mich.	Six-year-old Kayla Rolland shot dead at Buell Elementary School near Flint, Mich. The assailant was identified as a six-year-old boy with a .32-caliber handgun.
March 2000 Branneburg, Germany	One teacher killed by a 15-year-old student, who then shot himself. The shooter has been in a coma ever since.
March 10, 2000 Savannah, Ga.	Two students killed by Darrell Ingram, 19, while leaving a dance sponsored by Beach High School.
May 26, 2000 Lake Worth, Fla.	One teacher, Barry Grunow, shot and killed at Lake Worth Middle School by Nate Brazill, 13, with .25-caliber semiautomatic pistol on the last day of classes.
Sept. 26, 2000 New Orleans, La.	Two students wounded with the same gun during a fight at Woodson Middle School.
Jan. 17, 2001 Baltimore, Md.	One student shot and killed in front of Lake Clifton Eastern High School.
Jan. 18, 2001 Jan, Sweden	One student killed by two boys, ages 17 and 19.
March 5, 2001 Santee, Calif.	Two killed and 13 wounded by Charles Andrew Williams, 15, firing from a bathroom at Santana High School.
March 7, 2001 Williamsport, Pa.	Elizabeth Catherine Bush, 14, wounded student Kimberly Marchese in the cafeteria of Bishop Neumann High School; she was depressed and frequently teased.
March 22, 2001 Granite Hills, Calif.	One teacher and three students wounded by Jason Hoffman, 18, at Granite Hills High School. A policeman shot and wounded Hoffman.
March 30, 2001 Gary, Ind.	One student killed by Donald R. Burt, Jr., a 17-year-old student who had been expelled from Lew Wallace High School.
Nov. 12, 2001 Caro, Mich.	Chris Buschbacher, 17, took two hostages at the Caro Learning Center before killing himself.
Jan. 15, 2002 New York, N.Y.	A teenager wounded two students at Martin Luther King Jr. High School.
Feb. 19, 2002 Freising, Germany	Two killed in Eching by a man at the factory from which he had been fired; he then traveled to Freising and killed the headmaster of the technical school from which he had been expelled. He also wounded another teacher before killing himself.

April 26, 2002 Erfurt, Germany	13 teachers, two students, and one policeman killed, ten wounded by Robert Steinhaeuser, 19, at the Johann Gutenberg secondary school. Steinhaeuser then killed himself.
April 29, 2002 Vlasenica, Bosnia-Herzegovina	One teacher killed, one wounded by Dragoslav Petkovic, 17, who then killed himself.
April 14, 2003 New Orleans, La.	One 15-year-old killed, and three students wounded at John McDonogh High School by gunfire from four teenagers (none were students at the school). The motive was gang-related.
April 24, 2003 Red Lion, Pa.	James Sheets, 14, killed principal Eugene Segro of Red Lion Area Junior High School before killing himself.
Sept. 24, 2003 Cold Spring, Minn.	Two students are killed at Rocori High School by John Jason McLaughlin, 15.
Sept. 28, 2004 Carmen de Patagones, Argentina	Three students killed and 6 wounded by a 15-year-old Argentininan student in a town 620 miles south of Buenos Aires.
March 21, 2005 Red Lake, Minn.	Jeff Weise, 16, killed grandfather and companion, then arrived at school where he killed a teacher, a security guard, 5 students, and finally himself, leaving a total of 10 dead.
Nov. 8, 2005 Jacksboro, Tenn.	One 15-year-old shot and killed an assistant principal at Campbell County High School and seriously wounded two other administrators
Aug. 24, 2006 Essex, Vt.	Christopher Williams, 27, looking for his ex-girlfriend at Essex Elementary School, shot two teachers, killing one and wounding another. Before going to the school, he had killed the ex-girlfriend's mother.
Sept. 13, 2006 Montreal, Canada	Kimveer Gill, 25, opened fire with a semiautomatic weapon at Dawson College. Anastasia De Sousa, 18, died and more than a dozen students and faculty were wounded before Gill killed himself.
Sept. 26, 2006 Bailey, Colo.	Adult male held six students hostage at Platte Canyon High School and then shot and killed Emily Keyes, 16, and himself.
Sept. 29, 2006 Cazenovia, Wis.	A 15-year-old student shot and killed Weston School principal John Klang.
Oct. 3, 2006 Nickel Mines, Pa.	32-year-old Carl Charles Roberts IV entered the one-room West Nickel Mines Amish School and shot 10 schoolgirls, ranging in age from 6 to 13 years old, and then himself. Five of the girls and Roberts died.

Reprinted with permission from Information Please, www.infoplease.com, ©2006 Pearson Education, Inc.

General Procedures to Follow During a Crisis

- Follow specified procedures and be sure to use the District Crisis Intervention Manual, if one exists.
- Remain calm and in control. Do not panic.
- Do not leave your assigned area, which might include locking down other individuals with you.
- Only evacuate the building under police guidance, which is different than in previous training.
- If you have access to keys, blueprints, or maps—take them with you to the designated relocation center if escorted by police. You might consider having these under password protection on your web site. It is also a good idea to have copies housed at the first responders' offices—these will be the firemen and policemen.
- Take time to immediately document what you saw and did. Just the facts are needed. Keep emotions out if it and record it sequentially.

In Appendix A, there is an example of a crisis manual with numerous crisis procedures.

Handling of Hazardous Materials and Germ Warfare

There are many potential types of crisis in schools, but one of the areas that school districts may not have as much information on is the area of Hazardous Materials, and Chemical and Germ Warfare. The following is list of suggested steps to take in such an event:

Three I's of First Response

- **Identify** the material.
- **Isolate** area and keep others away.
- **Inform** proper authorities.
- If an unusual odor is detected, get up-wind of it as soon as possible if outside.
- Call 911 to get it checked by the experts.
- If itching occurs, shower with water with clothes on.
- Keep calm while waiting for the first responders.
- In the case of chemical & biological exposure, Fire Department and Health officials may need to quarantine.

Terms to know:
- A **chemical incident** is defined as the release of toxic chemicals often from industrial sites that are often capable to do bodily harm.
- A **biological incident** is defined as the release of bacteria, viruses, and/or toxins that could cause bodily harm.
- A **radiological incident** is defined as the release or exposure to radiological materials that are capable to do bodily harm.

Why Terrorists Target Schools

According to the Secret Service, schools may face the possibility of terrorist attacks. It is important to note that a terrorist can be a neighbor who has intense beliefs on agricultural issues, animal rights, abortion, and the environment. For example, in the Cokeville, Wyoming incident, the terrorists were a former policeman and his wife, who were right-wing, home-grown terrorists. Schools are a likely target, according to the Secret Service, who has reported that there is increased "chatter" about schools as targets by terrorists.

Why would terrorists target schools? Schools are soft targets, and are easy to get into. Incidents in schools garner considerable and immediate media attention. Terrorism in schools grips parents with fear, causing significant national and international reactions.

It would be relatively easy to use bombs, take hostages, or introduce bio-terrorism into the systems.

Another reason why schools may be potential targets is further reinforced by a national survey. In the 2002 National Survey of School Resource Officers, it was found that 95% of responding school-based police officers indicated that their schools were vulnerable to terrorist attacks, with 79% stating that their schools were not adequately prepared for such attacks. School officers also reported significant gaps in school security and emergency preparedness measures at their schools, adding that they had limited training and support for preventing and preparing terrorist attacks on schools. In the 2003 National Survey of School Resource Officers, over 90% of those surveyed believed that schools were "soft targets" for potential terrorist attacks. Over 76% of the officers felt that their schools were not adequately prepared to respond to a terrorist attack upon their schools, and over 51% of the respondents' schools did not have specific, formal guidelines to follow when there was a change in the national homeland security color code/federal terrorism warning system. According to these police officers, there is a great deal of work to be done.

Possible Terrorist Threat: Bio-Terrorism

Prior to the incident where assassins used fire alarms to get entire student bodies out of buildings so they could shoot them, it was normal to move all people out of buildings. On March 24, 1998 in Jonesboro, Arkansas, this standard procedure for evacuating buildings in a crisis was forever changed. In the Jonesboro situation, the false fire alarm was deliberately and falsely used to get the student body to evacuate so that the shooters could open fire on them as they exited the building. In a crisis, other than in the case of fire, there are very few reasons why people should be moved out of buildings unless specifically directed to do so by local law enforcement. In most crises, it is recommended to shelter in place.

The following is the recommended procedure for sheltering in place while awaiting first responders in a bio-chemical incident:

- Move students inside the building immediately, have a plan to get students off the playground.
- Close all the building openings, vents, windows and doors. Lock windows to achieve a tighter seal.
- Turn off heating and cooling ventilation systems. Turn thermostats to off, close dampers on ventilation and heating systems.
- Move students / staff to designated rooms and seal rooms. Plastic and duct tape have been suggested, but use whatever is available to seal off any openings. Clothing could be used to help seal gaps around doors or windows.
- Turn on a radio, if possible, to monitor emergency announcements. Stay in a lockdown until told that it is clear. If the classrooms have a computer, turn them on for information shared via email.

A school district must always be prepared to follow the first responders guide when dealing with any situation. The hazardous materials team, likely from the fire department, will have specific steps they will follow in the case of such an incident. It is advisable to plan with the local authorities when preparing for any possible crisis.

Possible Terrorist Threat: Bombs

When a bomb threat is called in, there are steps that the person talking to the threatening individual should do. A check list is recommended for everyone who would be taking calls. Ask everyone in that position to have this ready in case they are needed to help identify the caller. It is wise to have a list like the following printed and by every phone in the district:

Bomb Threat Check-Off List

Describe Caller's Voice		
		Male
		Female
		Calm
		Agitated
		Young
		Middle-aged
		Old
		American
		Accent
		Disguised
		Sure
		Unsure
		Giggling
		Slow
		Fast
		Loud
		Stuttering
		Lisping
		Angry
		Crying
Ask where the bomb is located.		
Ask what the bomb looks like.		
Ask when it is set to detonate.		
Ask why they placed the bomb in the school.		
Did the caller sound familiar? How?		
Was there any background noise? If so, what was it?		
Did the caller answer when you calmly asked them who they are and where they are? (When agitated they may forget and give this to you.)		

If a bomb threat is found in any written format (either on a note or on a restroom mirror), the note should be saved or photographed clearly so that the handwriting can be compared. Another important caution is to be sure that the note is not cleaned off (e.g. on a restroom mirror or blackboard) by a well-intentioned custodian before the evidence is documented.

If there are security cameras around the area where the note was found, the video or digital records should be examined for possible evidence or suspicious persons.

It is important to ensure that all witnesses have been thoroughly interviewed with accurate and complete documentation. Once the validity of the threat is determined, then the police should be brought into the investigation. It will then be best to follow the crisis plan for bomb threats in the decision whether to close school or evacuate. In most cases there is no real likelihood of a bomb, but if there is a history of repeated threats, the districts will probably evacuate or dismiss school.

Procedure for the Aftermath of a Crisis

After the crisis is over, there is a need for a follow-up plan. Some general guidelines include:

- Avoid spreading rumors and avoid talking where someone might overhear you.
- Do not talk with the media, but if there is a media contact in the district, leave it to them. One consistent message is important.
- Reduce psychological suffering. Engage counselors immediately, using debriefing strategies to determine which staff and students need further counseling.
- Help get the system back to normal as soon as possible.
- Continue with all duties as soon as possible.
- Avoid confusion.
- Avoid potential liability—people need to be where they are supposed to be and do what they have been instructed to do.
- Help maintain a supportive, positive environment. Encourage everyone to help others.
- Discourage memorials within educational buildings.

Documentation

Forms of documentation include surveillance camera digital images; written documentation; still photographs, audiotapes, actual artifacts, student management records, and police records. In the case of any school crisis, documentation is crucial. It not only helps in determining the outcome of the event, but it is also important in any litigation that would follow. Another reason is that under the No Child Left Behind (NCLB) Act, schools need to report if they are persistently dangerous. The three requirements dealing with crisis under the law, that are reportable, are as follows:

1. Victim of a violent crime while on the grounds.

2. Must be student related. (If a principal gets shot, it is not considered a reportable incident, but if a student gets shot, it is. All of this will eventually be determined in court.)
3. Must transfer students if requested to do so IF school is labeled persistently dangerous. (This is defined by each state.)

Communication and Other Crises

The communications system is a vital component of the safety and security system of the school. This becomes all the more important during a crisis. How does the district communicate between offices, buildings, and between buildings and the central office? How does the district use computers? Is technology a growing medium of teaching? Is learning through Alternative Service Providers offered over the Internet? In most cases, school districts are indeed increasing their daily reliance on business applications and the Internet.

A continuity plan needs to be in place if the district relies on communication via the Internet. It is critical to have a backup plan to continue communication if this service is damaged or interrupted, or if the service ceases for some reason during a crisis. Major companies like IBM have full divisions set up that can restore damaged communication and business systems in a matter of hours. How would it be done in your district?

Do you have backup data storage systems? Is there access to alternative Internet services immediately? How many days would a district or building be down if there was damage done to the technology systems in that building? Districts could make cooperative arrangements with other districts or agencies to assure continuance of communication. A centralized educational agency like an Area Educational Agency could be the backup.

One way that many districts are bolstering their security is by the addition of surveillance cameras in their buildings. Not only do they tend to make a more secure learning environment, but the return on investment is high since both students and the general public are attracted to classes and events held in a safe and secure environment. Just controlling vandalism can justify costs.

To ensure that campuses stay secure, administrators along with their safety and security department personnel might want to consider designing, developing, and implementing a strategic plan that details proactive ways to prevent crimes and protect assets. In order to ensure safe schools, a Security & Loss Prevention Plan is an excellent reference for school administrators and school safety and law enforcement personnel for creating safe and secure academic environments. Does your district have one?

Throughout the nation, school officials are debating whether to install surveillance cameras as part of their security systems. Some school systems already have them scanning the hallways while others debate the importance of adding them to schools. Some favor the electronic eyes to keep students and teachers safe, guard against vandalism and theft, or prevent forbidden behavior such as smoking.

Surveillance cameras are mainly used for one reason: to ensure safety within a specific area. Surveillance cameras are used in stores, places of business, schools, etc.; however, the use of surveillance cameras in schools has also become a controversial subject over privacy. "We felt a little bit like that was Big Brother watching, so we don't believe in having them in our schools." This quote from a teacher illuminates how some people feel that security cameras are intrusive.

That said, this very notion about "Big Brother watching" can lead to people to think twice about causing harm—since they are constantly being watched and recorded, they know they will not be able to talk their way out of taking responsibility for their actions. Cameras provide proof, and students will not be able to blame other students because the evidence will be on tape. Having cameras decreases the incidence of vandalism and consequently, schools are spared the expense of repairing the damage. Cameras are also a constant eye that never blinks—while employing security guards is a good idea, they are likely to miss out on certain activities because they cannot possibly watch everything at once. Security camera systems can be expensive, but they pay for themselves in just a few months.

Metal detectors are another form of security equipment used in some schools. New York City piloted a program, which has been expanded due to its success, in identifying students with weapons. Metal detectors are very expensive, and they need to be maintained by those with proper expertise. Despite these high costs, metal detectors have been shown to be very effective. In a study conducted in 1989 called the National Adolescent Student Health Survey, it was found at that time that over 100,000 students carried guns to school. Districts need to consider that it is likely that students in their districts carry or have carried guns to school. Metal detectors may be considered in some areas as essential to the safety and security of the buildings.

The processing, storage and serving of school food is also a safety concern. Given the heightened risk of bio-terrorism, it is critical to ensure that no unauthorized person has access to the food products. The Bureau of Nutritional Programs and School Transportation is a good source for more information on this topic.

When developing crisis plans, consideration should be given to student and staff health concerns such as the ever increasing number of students who have asthma. In some districts, they have received grants to get epi-pins for every nurse's office. Defibrillators have also been added to the standard safety equipment of many schools. In a crisis, the district can then assist students immediately and likely save lives, or at the very least decrease the anxiety involved for the affected student.

Technology crises can range from merely not having access to the Internet to the intentional disabling of delivery systems by people with intent to harm. Scammers, computer viruses, and system failures are all a huge concern for any school district. Areas that need to be considered when creating a safety plan for technology would be backup systems storage, compliance with requirements and laws, availability of tape encryption, and updating staff training with the constantly changing technology. The goal for a district may be to have a duplicate system, a system that is completely identical to ensure complete backup in case of an emergency. There should be a means to get the system up and running almost seamlessly since more and more schools rely on computer systems for business, teaching and learning, finance, human resources, and communications.

Communication during a regular day is crucial to the business of schooling, but in a crisis, it becomes all the more critical. The tense situation that evolves in a crisis leads to rumors that can lead to potential panic. All systems of communication, whether telephone or email, are essential in handling a crisis. Communication between agencies in a crisis needs to be seamless. Contacting law enforcement officers in a secure fashion so that people with scanners cannot intercept the call for help will result in less community panic. Parents and students could be contacted via automated telephone or mass email, reducing the immediate tasks for those handling the crisis.

Teachers in a lockdown situation could communicate very easily if the email system is running; this would help with the uncertainty of holding large numbers of students for any length of time. For example, if the classrooms had been locked down for a couple hours, there would be concerns about bathroom issues and possibly medication needs. Many times in a crisis, the police require an extended full lockdown where no one moves from the classroom, but once they have the crisis cordoned off to one location, limited movement might be allowed for students to go to the bathroom as long as they do not have full access to the school. Without authorizing full activity, an email message could allow some activity in limited areas of the school. Communication could be controlled, making it safer for all involved.

Chapter Two

School District Preparation for Crisis

In this chapter, discussion and exploration will focus on:

- How Crisis Planning is conducted
- Creation and Duties of the Safety and Security Steering Committees
- Crisis Manual Creation
- Facility Audits
- Drill and Practice Procedures
- Continuity Planning
- Checklist for a Safer District

The discussion about the vast potential of possible crisis scenarios may understandably be overwhelming. It would therefore be helpful to sort and organize the actions that should be taken. Using a step-by-step planning procedure, our ability on how to rise to the occasion becomes less abstract and more concrete.

How Crisis Planning is Conducted

Let's assume that the district has no up-to-date safety and/or security plans. They may have fire escape maps in every room and have been doing regular fire drills. There is paperwork on what to do in case of a tornado and/or a hurricane, but other than these basic requirements, there have been no concerted efforts to focus on anything other than teaching and learning. A new district administrator has been hired and holds the vision to create a district that is better prepared against school hazards and threats of the present day.

What is to be done first? Completing a district audit of what actually is presently being done would be the first step. There may be a particular school that has made more steps toward security plans than others. Who is that team of people who have taken it on? What plans have they made for their particular school? This could be a starting benchmark.

Once the audit is completed, a project plan should be created. The plans should address issues such as:

- What needs to be accomplished and under what timeline?
- Is it a facilities safety audit or the creation of a crisis manual or training for staff? Is it all inclusive?
- How much time will it take to finish one aspect?
- What is of top priority?

In most cases, this will result in the creation of a crisis manual so that in the event of a crisis there are procedures that everyone understands and knows to follow. These procedures should be easily accessible and quickly referred to while in the midst of the crisis. In the project plan, it is critical to include timelines, so that benchmarks will be noted and recognized. The massive challenge of creating and organizing a systematic plan to increase safety and security in schools can be very discouraging if small steps are not met and recognized.

A beginning plan for the lead administrator may look like the following:

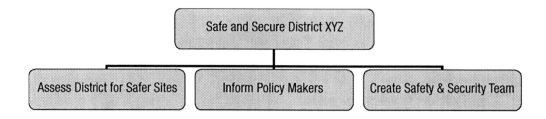

Under "Assess District for Safer Sites," details on each building and a date for each visit should be recorded to determine the status of drills, safety signage, and other work completed for a safer learning environment. While at each site, it would be good to scout for staff members who would be effective members on the district safety steering committee. These individuals should be encouraged to volunteer.

Under "Inform Policy Makers", tasks such as discussing with the Superintendent about the lead administrator on this effort should be included. A memo to the Board of Education should be the next step to ensure that they are aware of this administrative plan and will therefore be able to answer questions from the staff and/or community. Talk to the administrators in a general meeting to discuss the need and purpose for this effort. Record their ideas and request volunteers for the steering committee.

Finally, the creation and duties of the Safety and Security Steering Committee should be drawn up. Once the members are selected, a plan with a timeline and benchmarks should be set in place so that the committee has their tasks and expectations laid out. The Safety and Security Steering Committee could include members from the community, but they are usually representatives from the district.

Assuming that the steering committee decides to tackle the creation of a crisis manual, sub-committees should then be created to conduct the research with other districts— one to research outside agencies, one to develop recommendations for the community collaboration members, and one to complete the writing and editing.

Additional committees could also be created as needed by the local district. For instance, if there are a lot of major plants that handle hazardous materials in the surrounding area, there may be a committee that deals with only that issue. It would be a good idea to look at the community first, and then determine what the most likely crises are based on the environment. Those crisis procedures would be best created with the help of the safety officers from those plants or other agencies based on where the school district is located.

Crisis Manual Creation

When the area survey is completed, and the community members are initiated and involved, the next step is to determine which procedures apply to that particular school district. If the committee has made recommendations to include "Intruders in Schools" but not to include "Act of War," then the whole committee needs to agree on that. What needs to be in the manual and how the manual will be designed is a group decision that will eventually be recommended for official approval. Once officially approved by the Board of Education, it becomes a document that needs to be followed, so agreement from as many players as possible is essential.

The actual document could be as simple as a three ring-binder with a procedure on each page, so that in the case of a crisis, the administrator can tear the procedure from the book and use it as a checklist. It can then be replaced very easily. This design also lends itself to changing procedures if it is uncovered after use that steps need to be altered. It also could be placed on the web, and/or a digital file that can be accessed by the authorities.

No matter what format the Safety and Security Committee decides to use, it is important that the creation of the crisis manual is seriously considered from a local viewpoint, not just copied from another district's crisis manual. It needs to reflect the environment of the district and the capabilities of the local first responders. An example of this is if the district is very rural and there are no hazardous materials teams in the sheriff's department, a plan on what to do in that crisis would be different than if the district were urban with first responders and various crisis teams available.

It is important to ensure that the committee members represent all agencies that will have impact on a school crisis. These include the police, fire and sheriff departments, the Emergency Management System personnel, representatives from the Chamber of Commerce, City Council and the School Board. Other agencies that can be of great help are the County Health Department, American Red Cross, the Salvation Army, Family and Human Service, as well as hospital representatives. Another very helpful resource is representatives from the funeral homes who can help with grief issues and dealing with the requirements and procedures in case of multiple deaths. The very first responders in a school crisis also need to be at the meeting, and these would be the teachers, custodians, administrators and counselors.

Once a creative team of interested people gets working, more ideas will be generated. It is very important to keep the efficacy of the team positive by setting small steps, announcing the accomplishments, and ensuring they are put to use throughout the district. Assuming that the crisis manual has been agreed upon and the team has presented it for approval to the school board, a date for district wide distribution and training should be set. If the district has approved a crisis manual, it is imperative that everyone follow it in the event of an emergency from that point on. The liability increases if a plan is in place, and a school or employee chooses not to use it.

The completion of the manual should be cause for celebration at the next general meeting, with its uses carefully explained to everyone. The administrators will learn from each other as they use it, and most of them will be very positive about having a simple, step-by-step procedure in a time of stress. If a debriefing is done in major administrative meetings as the crisis manual is used, it will solidify the importance of its use to the administrators since it will show them how the manual can help them in a crisis.

Facility Audits

Once the crisis manual is in place, the next step is to conduct a facility audit. A complete analysis of the buildings is required to determine how the entire district can be made more secure. Many years ago, school districts were simply concerned with whether doors were locked. Many issues we need to contend with today did not exist; for example, the donation of a tree blocking the line of sight into the school in the event of a crisis was not a consideration. Evacuation in and out of a building traditionally was simply the door, with no additional exit routes considered, e.g. windows. Now an additional, alternative route needs to be in place. In order to ensure that school districts have comprehensively examined all the facility safety concerns, it is recommended they conduct some type of facility review. One such system of auditing is called a Crime Prevention through Environmental Design (CPTED) audit.

Crime Prevention through Environmental Design (CPTED) Audits can be coordinated with trained police officers. Contact the local department to see if they have anyone who has been trained. They will often do this without charge. If there is no one available, more information on this can be found on the following web site: http://www.nicp.net/ (The National Institute of Crime Prevention). Proper design and effective use of the built environment can lead to a reduction in the incidence of crime. This prevention strategy is discussed further in Chapter Three.

Assuming that the CPTED audits for school buildings have been conducted, a list of suggestions made by the auditors on improving the safety of the environment should be carefully studied. Some suggestions can be as simple as trimming bushes to allow a clean line of sight outside the buildings to adding security cameras in areas that are difficult to monitor. Other areas for possible improvement include fencing, exterior lighting, portable classroom security, chemical storage and playground improvements. There are also other important issues that need to be addressed, such as building access control. Who has the keys and how are they controlled? Are the alarms working properly? Are the classroom chemicals stored properly? Roof access and possible access may need to be modified. Once the list has been created, select the suggestions that are the least expensive and get those implemented as soon as possible. The other ideas may need to be added to a facilities planning improvement document for the district and be completed as the money becomes available.

Each building in any school district is unique. For example, factors that make each building unique include the neighborhood it is located in, the style of architecture, and the age of the structure. It is important to require that the school safety committees keep abreast of changes and renew their plans and actions accordingly.

There should be alternative sites in case evacuation is necessary. Suggestions are provided in the crisis manual at the end of this book for this. Once the building plan is created, it is critical to revisit it annually so that new staff know what to do and to reinforce the district's priority on safety. A requirement that every principal file an annual report to the district would help formalize the school plans and emphasize their importance.

Another common suggestion by the safety committee is the requirement that all staff wear identification badges, and that all doors have working locks. There may be recommendations that some of the older buildings in the district need new doors that are securable. Other suggestions that usually come from committees include conducting drills and more staff training. Once the list of suggestions has been created, the committee can prioritize the list and create a timeline for each task.

Financing any safety improvements can be a roadblock to accomplishing these improvements. There are many safety grants, some of which were created specifically to improve facilities. Grants are one suggestion, but any district budget line items that deal with facility improvement could be used to improve security in the district. District budgets are often very small with large needs, so awareness and ownership among the stakeholders is important to generate support for the use of general education funds to improve safety.

Drill and Practice Procedures

One of the least expensive ways of increasing safety in schools is to improve drill and practice procedures. It can be as simple as doing paper-and-pencil, desk top drills; these usually consist of written scenarios where teams of teachers or administrators sit together to discuss what they would do in their building if a designated crisis incident happened. For example, teams of people could be asked to imagine three scenarios and then determine what their role would be in each and share that with their team.

The schools could also try an all-call to lock down in place with a code or just by an announcement over the intercom that everyone is to lock down. Once this announcement is made, a check should be made on the time it took for every area to be secured and if everybody took the drill seriously. The findings should be discussed at the next staff meeting, and any suggestions for improvement should be noted and incorporated into the individual building plans. Improvement ideas usually result from asking critical questions, such as who is to check the restrooms for students, where do they go in a lockdown, who checks the parking lot or playground, and so on. Many important ideas for improvements come from drills because they bring to light issues that would not usually be noticed.

Another type of drill can be carried out by working with the local authorities. They need the training as much as the schools, and are very willing to do a mock intruder/

hostage situation so that their SWAT team can be called in to train. The local police or sheriff's office may want to do this without letting their teams know it is a drill. It is suggested that the schools do this type of drill when students are not present since the image of black-clad, heavily armed officers charging in could cause great alarm to the students. It has been noted in drills of this type that even if the staff knows it is a practice drill, there still is a great deal of apprehension. After the drill, it is an opportune learning experience to debrief both the officers and the staff. Both teams will learn much from each other in these cases.

If the district has a solid relationship with the local emergency planning committees, there may be opportunity to do a full drill involving all first responders. One such practice drill might be a bio-hazard attack. If this is held when students are not in session, the high school drama students could possibly act as victims. This type of drill will bring in the fire department, the local police, and the media, involve the hospitals and possibly major military bio-terrorism squadrons. The different groups need the experience, and training with the schools only adds to the effectiveness. The debriefing after such a drill often takes place off the school site under the incident commander's guidance.

One requirement that is difficult for many school administrators to follow—but must be enforced—is that once a call has been made to 911 and the first responders are on site, the first responders are in charge. This is because the site could be considered a crime scene, but more importantly, it is essential that there is only one person in charge of the crisis—the incident commander. An incident commander comes with the first response vehicle, which is often the fire department. It should be noted that this person does not necessarily remain the incident commander through the entire crisis since the designation could change as demanded by the changing conditions of the crisis.

The district and school administrators' role in such a crisis is to be supportive of their needs. They may need maps, lists of students in attendance that day, access points that are not obvious and many other questions that will come up. The administrators are not in their normal role as the one responsible and while it can be difficult to give up that role, it is critical to remember that the incident commander is counting on the strong support of the administrators to ensure that the process moves as smoothly as possible.

One safety measure that could be considered is to provide all building administrators with handheld devices that allow Internet access or have a program that holds an accurate listing of staff and students as well as their contact details. These devices are easy to keep up-to-date by downloading daily from the district student management system, and they would work on their backup batteries if the systems went down during a crisis. It would also help to have cameras and camcorders on hand for a crisis so that the events can be recorded. This would be very helpful in answering questions later and providing documentation of the incident.

There are so many different scenarios that can be used in drills, much more so than the allocated time to practice. One important scenario that most schools have not practiced yet is one of bio-terrorism. To conduct such a drill, a possible scenario could be one where a smoking cylinder is found in one of the high school classrooms. A teacher is lying face down by the object. Once that is discovered and the call is made to 911, what does a school do? It should be able to refer to its High School Crisis Manual under Hazardous Materials and Bio-Terrorism for step-by-step procedures.

In the planning, there needs to be clear roles assigned and drilled. Who would go to the hospital if someone were injured? Who oversees the telephones and computer databases? Who works with the media, and who would do it if the assigned person were not there during the crisis? Has the media been informed that they will not be allowed on site during any crisis but that they can receive information from the assigned central location on a regular and timely basis? How will the parents and family of the injured be notified, and who is responsible for that? In a major crisis, would there need to be an administrator assigned to work with the Emergency Management Service people at their site?

Continuity Planning

Continuity planning is important. How will the district get a school up and running if a facility burns to the ground? If an earthquake hits, how will the communication systems be augmented or replaced, and how quickly could that be accomplished? In continuity planning, there are a few steps that need to be considered. There is a need for immediate action often completed with 12 hours of the event.

Step one involves assessing damages and injuries, striving to establish as normal an environment as possible, and the activation of alternative plans.

Step two is the initial recovery, which happens often in the first two days. A comprehensive assessment of damage and injuries is addressed at this time, along with establishing further connections with outside agencies. Memorials and/or funerals should have district representation.

Step three involves repairing the damage from the crisis. Establishment of an alternative site for the rest of the school year may be needed. Ongoing counseling needs should be assessed and fulfilled.

Step four is the re-opening of the facility. This could be immediately or many months later. It is wise to not have permanent memorials on school sites, but many times administrators are pressured to have such events. Having a policy in place prior to a crisis would help make those decisions.

Training is not just drilling with local authorities, but also keeping skills up-to-date for blood pathogen, hazardous materials handling, CPR (Cardio-Pulmonary Resuscitation), first aid, etc. It is also critical to ensure that there is continual updating of the Crisis Manual following a discussion after its use. After each use of the Crisis Manual, debrief with the administrator in charge, and ask if there are suggestions for change. These suggestions should be relayed to the safety committee, and the changes implemented if they are recommended. Continuous learning as procedures are applied to actual crises is of great importance.

Checklist toward a Safer District

This district could report making great strides toward a safer school environment if the following conditions are met:

- There is a working district safety committee
- There is an approved and used District Crisis Manual
- Each building has a safety plan which includes an evacuation plan
- Each classroom has locks that can be activated from the inside, and there are working communication devices in all classrooms
- Staff members and visitors wear badges when on any district site
- The facility audits have been completed, and suggestions have been addressed
- There have been numerous drill and practices on various types of crises
- Staff members are aware of suspicious activity and report it immediately
- Administrators conduct debriefing with each other and with staff whenever the Crisis Manual is used

It is vital that each school site has a plan of action during an evacuation.

It is important to check if each building has:

- An evacuation kit which may include distinguishing badges or vest for those in charge?
- A way to identify students who are injured with tags before they are transported to the hospitals?
- A list of all students in every class with emergency telephone numbers?
- A sign-out sheet for parents picking students up from an alternative site?
- Some simple first aid materials?
- A bull horn or other communication device for large crowds?
- Important emergency numbers for other agencies?
- A list of staff and student health concerns?
- And anything else that could easily be carried in a box or backpack quickly to an evacuation site?

The quest to improve school safety is an ongoing process, and there will always be something that should be done. If the district does not have security cameras, for instance, this may be the next goal. Grants could be written to obtain them for every building. It is suggested that security cameras should be made available in every building. Financing is a concern, but if there is a plan in place to give a base number of cameras to every building and the district adheres to the plan as money allows, it will reduce the legal liability if a concern happens in a building that has not yet installed their cameras. Security cameras are extremely beneficial for all grade levels. They placate angry individuals and catch vandals. They lessen concerns with discipline and make the finalization of discipline concerns an easier reporting issue. It is hard to say, "My child would not do that," when their behavior is captured and shown on screen.

Another planning suggestion is to have offices for multiple administrators in different parts of the building. This would be beneficial in a situation where there is a hostage situation in one office; the administrators who are not trapped in the other office could then help in the crisis.

School Resource Officers are frequently hired as collaborative staff members with the local police force. In some districts, the Police Liaison or School Resource Officers are employees of the police force, but their assignment is to be in their assigned school every day that school is in session. Other districts use private security guards. One issue that may be coming to the district is whether to allow the security force to carry tazers in the schools. This could be a volatile issue and needs to be handled carefully, although it seems to be a better solution to tazer a person out of control than to shoot them with a gun.

It is likely that other law enforcement equipment that will come up in suggestions by the department and new types of crises will crop up as the years go by. As mentioned earlier, the school safety plans did not include bio-terrorism 20 years ago. Safety and security has to be a continuous effort and is ever changing. The one constant that will prevail is the need to be prepared.

Chapter Three

Crisis Prevention

In this chapter, discussion and exploration will focus on:

- Facility Audit
- Crime Potential
- Threat Assessments
- Interviewing Potential Violent Students

Facility Audit

CPTED (Crime Prevention through Environmental Design) Audits can be coordinated with trained police officers. The first step is to call the local department to see if they have anyone who has been trained. They will often do this for no charge. If there is no one available, more information on this can be found on the following web site: http://www.nicp.net/ (The National Institute of Crime Prevention). Proper design and effective use of the built environment can lead to a reduction in crime, leading to a safer environment and an improvement in workplace quality.

CPTED is defined as "the proper design and effective use of the built environment that can lead to a reduction in the fear and incidence of crime and an improvement in the quality of life." The goal is to reduce opportunities for crime that may be inherent in the design of structures or in the design of neighborhoods. Cities and counties throughout the country are adopting ordinances requiring site plan reviews with crime prevention in mind. Law enforcement officers who are specially trained in CPTED are now working closely with planners, architects, city officials, and educators to ensure the proper design of structures, schools and neighborhoods.

The purpose of a CPTED audit is to learn how the design and use of the environment can control human/criminal behavior and reduce the fear of crime. It is a form of crime prevention through natural means. A major part of this audit is to show how natural access control and natural surveillance decrease the opportunity for crime. For example, school districts will learn from the audit the different aspects of lighting and its effects on human behavior. They will learn from the audit which areas of the schools need to have the foliage trimmed or designs reconfigured so there is a direct line of sight into any building in the event of a crisis.

Although the audits take quite some time—in larger districts, it could actually take a year to complete since the officers who have been trained are often assigned to other duties on the police force— the results of the audit are invaluable and worth waiting for. Areas that often are recommended for surveillance and improvements include:

Bushes that are too high and too close to buildings since they obstruct view into the building.

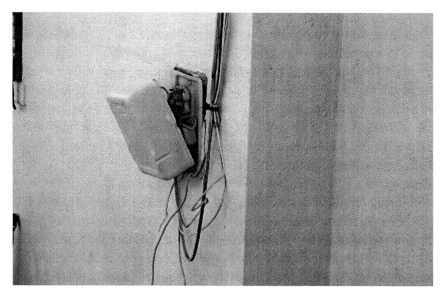

Unlocked utility sources which are accessible to anyone.

Utility areas should be enclosed in a locked space so that they are not accessible to unauthorized persons.

Playground and landscaping gravel should be examined as they can be used a destructive missiles.

Broken curb and crumbling cement can also be used for mischief by vandals.

The following are other suggestions to consider when focusing on safer school campuses.

- Where school grounds are concerned, consideration should be made on:
  o Poorly defined borders
  o Poor building layouts with isolated areas
  o No vehicular separation, e.g. buses and cars in the same place
  o Isolated areas near fields
  o Non-secured storage areas
  o Inadequate signage
  o Unsafe play equipment and ground surfacing
  o Allowing multiple entrances
  o Views obstructed by landscaping

Problems that are often found in schools are:

- Remote locations that are hard to monitor
- Unlocked entrances
- Isolated areas at the ends of hallways which could pose a security risk
- Graffiti allowed to remain on school buildings or structures
- Drop-in ceilings as such unsupervised areas could be possible areas for bomb placement.

CPTED audits are very helpful in getting a clear understanding of how to create a safer environment without initially spending a great deal of money. There are often suggestions that will take more time and money, but the initial recommendations can often be addressed by fixing doors or ensuring there are safety locks that work on utility doors or fences. Trimming bushes so that there is a direct line of sight and minimizing possible hiding places for harmful individuals or objects is a fairly inexpensive safety measure.

Crime Potential

Working with community partners will help school districts determine neighborhood crime incidents, pedophiles' addresses, drug activity around schools, and general incidence of malice toward others. Some school sites have far more concern that others, but to assume a crisis would not happen in a particular neighborhood is foolish. If a district is large, they need to expect the same preparation from every site, no matter where it is located.

Most school districts are using some sort of student management system. Often times, those systems can be utilized to gather information that will help with safety and security measures. The systems should be able to answer questions such as:

- How many students have been suspended and/or expelled in comparison to other years?
- Are there certain students that need to have a violence awareness review?
- Can the system tell who is failing in comparison to those who are truant?
- Does this have any connection to those who are being considered for a violence awareness review?
- What is the vandalism rate for individual school sites?
- Is there a need for more security cameras in specific spots to deter vandalism?

These student management systems are a valuable resource for identifying possible areas / persons of concern.

Threat Assessments

There are many areas to consider when thinking of preventative measures. One would be to do threat assessment training for those who would need to determine the level of a threat as in a bomb threat or a possible shooter. There are four types of threats that have been identified by the Secret Service:

1. A **direct threat** is one that clearly identifies a specific target and is delivered in a straightforward and explicit manner. An example might be: "I am going to drive my car, filled with bombs, into the front entrance of the gym during tonight's basketball game."
2. An **indirect threat** tends to be unclear. The plan is not specific nor is the victim or the motivation noted. An example of an indirect threat might be: "If I wanted to, I could shoot everyone in this school."

3. A **veiled threat** is a strongly stated warning of intention to do harm such as, "We would be better off if you were not our principal."
4. A **conditional threat** warns of a violent act that could happen if the demands are not met. For example, "If you don't call off the track meet, I will place bombs to go off at the finish line."

It would be a preventative measure for districts to train their staff to hear the differences in these types of threats. The low level is vague and indirect while the middle level threat is more direct and the wording indicates that the person threatening has given it some thought. The highest level is given in a direct manner and is specific as well as being plausible. It often has a specific target and a specific time. It has been found that many of these threats are from people who have access to the materials needed to do the crime. The direct threat is therefore of highest and immediate concern.

A threat assessment sheet on possible violent students would be a preventative measure—this was discussed previously in Chapter One.

Further traits to consider in determining possible criminal intent in a direct threat are:

Announces their intent	Shares thoughts through drawing, writing, and verbal intentions.
Low frustration tolerance	Student is often insulted and angered.
Poor coping skills	Has little ability to deal with criticism, disappointment, rejection and rejection.
Lack of resiliency	Is unable to bounce back from a frustrating or disappointing experience.
Failed love relationship	Can not accept or come to terms with rejection or the ending of a relationship.
Feels everyone is against them	Real or perceived injustices collect in them.
Signs of depression and/or narcissism	Shows signs of lethargy, fatigue and self absorption.
Alienation	Is separate form others, often is sad.
Lack of empathy and dehumanizes others	Inability to understand or concerned about others and treats people like objects.
Exaggerated sense of entitlement	Expects special treatment
Superiority Complex	Feels better and smarter than everyone else.
High need for attention	Positive or negative attention is sought.
Blames others	Refuses to take responsibility.
Masks low self-esteem	May be arrogant but avoids involvement.
Anger management concerns	Tends to lash out in temper.

Another preventative measure is to watch for students who are intolerant, have inappropriate humor, have a lack of trust, closed social group, rigid and opinionated, have a fascination with entertainment of a violent nature, have negative role models, and general behavior that supports their ability to be violent.

Family dynamics are another factor to consider:
*   Is there a turbulent parent-child relationship?
*   Do the parents or guardians seem to accept the pathological behavior for their child as natural?
*   Is there access to weapons?

- Does the student dominate decisions in the family?
- Is there no monitoring of the student's time by the family?

Other factors to take into consideration include:
- What has the history of this student been in academics, activities, and discipline? (Note: Not all violent students have histories of concerns with the schools.)
- Does the student take part in the school?
- Is the student involved in drugs or alcohol?
- Is there a possibility of a copycat effect from another school violent incident?

Interviewing Potential Violent Students

When talking with a prospective violent student, the following checklist of questions may be of help:

- What are the student's motives and goals?
- Have there been any communications suggesting ideas or intent to be violent?
- Has the student shown inappropriate interest in school attacks, weapons or mass violence?
- Has the student previously attacked anything, including animals?
- Does the student have the capacity to carry out a threat?
- Do they have access to weapons?
- Is the student acting depressed, hopeless or are they in despair?
- Does the student have at least one trusting relationship with one responsible adult?
- Does the student see violence as an acceptable way to solve problems?
- Have others indicated a concern about this student's potential for violence?
- Are there other indicators that may cause this student to be under suspicion?

If there are mostly positive responses to the questions above, then there is cause to have a counselor work with this student as well as to make connections with the home or even the police. Although school personnel are highly trained, it would be wise to get outside opinion on potential violent students not just to help them, but also to ensure that the chance of violent action is minimized. It is also important to document this effort.

There are many potential crisis situations that schools face today that were not even considered as possibilities ten years ago. There are no guarantees that all the best plans, training and preparation will deter crisis in schools, but if one should occur, the school district will at least be much more prepared to handle the situation as opposed to being caught off guard with no plan at all.

Chapter Four

Preparedness by Collaborating with Communities

In this chapter, discussion and exploration will focus on:

- Collaboration
- All-Inclusive Planning
- Methods of Communication
- Equipment Needs and Costs
- Security Cameras
- Steps in Getting Surveillance Systems Approved
- Drug Policies and Drug Dog Searches

Collaboration

To successfully prepare school communities without creating panic, school and public safety officials should be candid about the possibility of schools being struck by various crisis situations. Officials need to communicate possible crisis issues in a balanced and rational context, and educate their school communities on the roles that everyone plays in keeping schools and communities safe. As long as details that compromise security are not released, it is generally best to be open and communicative with all stakeholders.

School and public safety officials nationwide now proactively pursue prevention programs, security measures and emergency preparedness measures to prepare for a potential crisis in their schools. The failure to talk about the possibility of such incidents occurring and to take steps to prepare for such an occurrence would be considered negligence in the eyes of most educators, public safety officials, parents, media and courts. This is in contrast with the past, where not too many years ago, much of what was included in today's crisis prevention and preparation measures would have been considered intrusive and exclusive to parents. For example, just the simple requirement of signing in at the front office before entering the building can cause some people to react negatively. Although there may be resistance to prevention procedures, the district needs to be consistent about enforcing the procedures. It would be helpful to talk about the increased possibility of school crises in a calm, rational manner so that it does not generate panic, but instead reduces fear, improves preparedness, and increases understanding that a heightened awareness can be helpful in preventing potential crises.

Fear of school crises is best managed by education, communication and preparation, and not through denial.

- **Educate** school community members by defining the issues in the appropriate context. There is much greater acceptance of a plan when people learn and understand the rationale behind them.
- **Communicate** with school community members to discuss risk reduction and heightened security and emergency preparedness strategies. Work with all stakeholders in the community who will have a part to play in any school crisis. Communicate throughout the process with stakeholders so they are kept informed of the progress made in the schools.
- **Prepare** for both natural disasters and man-made acts of crime and violence by taking an "all-hazards" approach to school emergency planning. Have a crisis plan with specific strategies for every foreseeable crisis.

By continually involving the community partners in the progress of securing the school district, this will keep the issue on the forefront and keep the lines of communication open for future planning.

Working with all those involved also includes the true first responders to any school crisis—the teachers, administrators, school support staff, School Resource Officers, school security personnel and other professionals on the front lines when any emergency occurs in schools. It is strongly recommended to work hand-in-hand with them in emergency planning. The reality is that those working inside a school will be the ones immediately responding to and managing an emergency incident while police, fire, the Emergency Management System and other community first responders are en route.

The proper protocol to recognize an incident commander during a crisis therefore needs to be developed. Does this person come with a badge? In a smaller community, a name would help to know who will be in charge in case of an emergency. Planning this ahead would prevent some confusion during a crisis.

School officials will also be the individuals working with community first responders once they arrive and throughout the emergency incident. In fact, if an event occurs on the scale of the 9/11 terror attacks, school officials may be forced to manage a school-based emergency with minimal support from community first responders if these responders are tied up managing other aspects of the emergency elsewhere in the community and/or if they cannot get to the school. School officials will also be the individuals left to carry the school a long way through the recovery phase after an emergency. School districts will also be held responsible so it is important to work with the local authorities to ensure that the appropriate steps are taken if help from the first responders is not immediate

All-Inclusive Planning

Not withstanding, it is important to do all-inclusive planning. Working with the community agencies, such as the Emergency Management System personnel, will give a larger view of the issues involved in community safety. They work closely with the National Incident

Management System and Homeland Security. It may be discussed in a particular state that there is a requirement that school district crisis plans must be NIMS compliant. According to the Federal Department of Education, there are no requirements unless they are tied to a specialized grant in crisis planning such as Response to Emergency Crisis Management grants. It would be wise to check with individual states and, of course, any specialized requirements associated with any granting programs that a district pursues to ensure that those requirements are in place. The Federal Emergency Management Agency (FEMA) is very supportive of NIMS compliancy in crisis planning but as of the publication of this book, the Federal government suggests but does not require NIMS compliancy for public school districts. For more information, please call FEMA at 1-800-238-3358.

There are Federal standards that must be used in order to receive Federal funding. In order to receive federal preparedness funds (which are different then recovery funds), you must be NIMS compliant. NIMS compliancy does NOT affect recovery funds from FEMA. In order to be NIMS compliant, there are several items that a school district must do. These items include training, planning and exercises. Even if you do not participate or apply for these funds, it would be good for a school to go through the training so they have a better understanding on how emergency crews will respond. One area that these agencies have concentrated on since 9/11 is to standardize the use of the Incident Command System and the National Response Plan. It is recommended that those planning school security plans incorporate as much of that as possible into the district plan so that the school district plan uses the same terminology as is used in the community plan. An example of this would be using the label Incident Commander instead of Crisis Manager.

Other individuals / agencies who can be asked to help with school district crisis planning include funeral directors, family service personnel, the Red Cross, the Salvation Army, churches, Board of Health, police, sheriff and fire personnel, city council connections and the Chamber of Commerce. School personnel that have direct ownership to this issue are the administrators, maintenance and nutritional service staff, the bus manager, teachers, counselors and custodians. To avoid duplication of services, it is recommended that these school personnel, along with some of the members of the agencies mentioned, are present at the meeting so that everyone understands their roles and responsibilities in the event of a crisis.

When working and developing a cooperative crisis preparation plan, it is a good idea to create and distribute to the proper authorities maps and location of utility shut-offs on school sites. People who may need those very quickly might be the fire department or the S.W.A.T. team in case of a hostage situation. They may be able to get into the building through ventilation systems. Such information needs to be accessible within minutes of a crisis. These plans should be updated whenever there is a change in facilities, and they could be stored on a password protected web site or on CDs. A printout should also be kept in a safe place.

Building access for first responders is one issue, but alternative escape routes need to be considered as well. If a temporary wall had been built, for instance, would it be fairly easy to break through it from inside? This is the kind of information that needs to be available; during such critical times, it will help make important decisions that could possibly save lives.

Methods of Communication

Identifying methods of communication in case of a crisis is of prime importance. Every classroom needs two-way communication capabilities. Telephone access with outside line connections is vital. No school district has enough telephone lines, but along with cell phones, there needs to be a way to get information out to the responders. Some fax machines that have telephone capabilities can be used as an emergency line if the electricity is lost or cut. Providing those to schools would prevent the intense phone congestion concern during a crisis, especially if schools keep the line number confidential. They would be able to make outgoing calls without the line being tied up with frantic incoming calls.

Even today, there are school buildings that have no two-way audio communication devices connecting the classrooms with the front office. A simple telephone system or an intercom should be the bare minimum that any district should have. This will ensure a flow of communication between the classroom and the front office without someone having to step out physically.

Equipment Needs and Costs

There are all kinds of equipment needs, e.g.

- Security cameras are growing in importance in schools.
- Safety and evacuation kits help in the event of an evacuation or extended lockdown.
- Locks on every classroom and office door are important to help protect against intruders or shooters in schools.

These needs come with costs. There is always a concern for costs involved in any school related expenditure, but in the area of school security and emergency preparedness, the budget needs to recognize priorities, such as immediate communication devices in every classroom or installing security cameras. Not considering security to be an important part of the budget is counter to the world's direction of heightening security efforts and emergency preparedness at both public and private facilities. It does not make sense that at a time when our leaders have insisted and found the resources to increase funding for protecting airlines, bridges, monuments and even the hallways of Capitol Hill, they have simultaneously cut funding to protect the children and teachers in the "soft target" hallways of America's schools. Although budget cuts are a reality in many districts, there still needs to be a plan to inform all funding agencies of the increasing costs and needs for more security equipment and training.

Even in these times of shrinking budgets, there are still ways to make schools safer with less money. For example, a simple and effective communication method during a lockdown situation from inside a classroom using pieces of paper with specific colors could be developed. The principal or designee would be able to check the building quickly with this very simple system. Each classroom could have three small colored paper squares. A green piece of paper would be pushed under the door if everything is fine in that classroom and they are just waiting for the all-clear signal. A yellow piece of paper could be used if there is a problem with a student from bathroom needs to a potential asthmatic in the room. A red piece of paper would be pushed under the door to signal that an intruder was in the room (provided doing so would not jeopardize those inside). No colored papers would indicate that there was a need to get into that room right away because no signal was given.

Security Cameras

Some districts are considering the installation of security cameras as another deterrent to violence. There are several different types of security cameras. A few different types of security cameras are black-and-white security cameras, color security cameras, wireless security cameras, night vision security cameras and vandal resistant security cameras. Some cameras are covert, some as tiny as a lipstick and some even smaller. Some security cameras also allow remote access—these allow monitoring of the sites through an Internet connection.

Camera surveillance provides an extra eye for security personnel and is widely recognized as a powerful deterrent to crime. However, the low ambient lighting found in schools makes it difficult, if not impossible, to capture quality video documentation. To combat this problem, vendors have specifically designed cameras to capture sharp video images, even in nearly complete darkness. Cameras can deliver quality video no matter what the lighting environment.

Choosing the right cameras for the right spots is important. An example of this would be trying to put surveillance on a front door by shooting a camera at the entrance from inside. The lighting would likely give only shadowed images since it would be shooting against the outside light. There are cameras designed for that situation, which of course cost more, but there may also be a way to install it at a different angle.

What about the costs of maintenance of security camera equipment?

It is recommended that security cameras are professionally checked with a regular audit. This is to ensure that the images are as rich as possible and will record vital images when most necessary. Security camera equipment is generally very durable, as confirmed during the implosion of the Aladdin Hotel-Casino on April 27, 1998. Amidst the 30,000 tons of rubble, a security camera was found by the cleanup crew, and it was still working.

Another important consideration in the maintenance of security cameras is potential vandalism to the security cameras. If this is the case, a possible solution is a metal box designed to allow access to the camera only if a key is available. There are also ways to design security cameras systems to shoot through windows to capture the outside.

Capabilities of the camera systems need to be considered. It is recommended that the school districts add the remote monitoring feature to their systems. This will allow visual access to any building that has security cameras from another site. This could be the central office or the police department. This would mean that the images of the activities in the school can be viewed as they are unfolding and prompt more timely responses.

While some of these systems have a VCR where the images are transmitted and stored to VCR tape, others transmit images from cameras to a digital hard drive storage system. The latter is a better option because more storage space is saved and it is easier to search for specific incidents. Schools should look for a multi-channel video surveillance system that utilizes the most advanced digital video compression technologies to deliver the highest picture quality and video performance.

Steps in Getting a Surveillance System Approved

The following are steps for a district to start the process of having a surveillance system approved:

- Create a Surveillance School Board Policy and have it approved by the Board of Education.
- Determine criteria on which schools would have the cameras added first.
- Secure grants.
- Create RFP (request for proposal).
- Run the bid process.
- Award the bid and made sure the bid lasts for five years.
- Each principal can determine where to place the cameras.
- Have the placement design created by the vendor with input by the principals.
- Equipment needs to be ordered, installed and tested.
- The technology team configures them to the district network system.
- Establish remote access capabilities to every camera in the district.

The following are possible criteria that could be used to determine which sites get the cameras first:

- Determine the highest crime rate areas by schools in the community
- Consider district programming for most at-risk students
- Determine the highest vandalism rates per building
- Ability to make the biggest steps per year

- Keep to a minimum system at each site at first but add as the financing becomes available

Funding for any such effort can be daunting for any school district, but some suggestions to consider are as follows:

- Grants
- Safe & Drug Free Schools Funds
- Company Donations
- PTO donations
- Installer Donations

Drug Policies and Drug Dog Searches

Most districts have a no tolerance policy for any drug involvement. Schools should have a clear policy on the use of drugs and alcohol, and this should be carefully communicated to the students, parents and the community. As clearly as this no tolerance policy is communicated, it is an unfortunate reality that there is usually some degree of drug use. However, school districts can collaborate with the local community for a stronger enforcement of this no tolerance policy.

Schools can be sites for drug dog training after school hours. Some police officers have canine police that are trained to do drug searches. These dogs need to be trained on a regular basis since many departments are eager to have them drill in schools. Drug dog searches are legal in most states, but it is important to check with the school district about any concerns.

Searches using drug dogs during the day could be a non-intrusive and easy operation with the officers having the dogs search the parking lot, or a full-scale operation with lockdowns throughout the building as the officers search the entire premises. It is wise not to have the dogs near the students or any individuals around the school area. Once the dogs find any drugs, they are trained to react in a certain manner, at which point the officers take over the search.

It should be noted that dogs do not discern between student drug users and adult drug users. Since this is a case, school administrators should be prepared that a staff member who is using drugs could be uncovered during this process.

Communicating with the public that the schools are going to use drug dogs in the schools is a good idea. By making the community aware of this important collaborative effort reinforces the no drug tolerance policy of the school district. It also demonstrates the district's commitment and efforts to make schools safer.

Chapter Five

Responding to School Crises

In this chapter, we will discuss and explore various scenarios, and how they can be handled.

Scenario One: Student School Shooter

It was a beautiful spring morning and the elementary students were all out on the playground, enjoying their last few minutes before going into the building to start their school day. Two teachers were standing together watching the students and having a conversation. All of a sudden, there are three "pops", and one teacher asked the other if she thought that was a car backfiring. "Strange, you rarely hear that much any more," the other teacher commented.

The students from around the other side of the building start running toward the teachers, and they are screaming and saying unintelligibly something about the word "hurt." The teachers both run around to the other side of the playground and see two students lying on the ground. The teacher asks what is going on, but then students ignore her and run off in all sorts of directions. The other students are running everywhere, including across the street and off over the field.

The teachers have no way of communicating, so one teacher runs into the school asking for help while the other one heads for the students lying on the playground. When she gets there, she hears "pops" and sees gravel spraying up toward her. She kneels down with the students to see what she can do and finds out that they are both not breathing. Then all of a sudden, she feels a hot sensation in her side. She has been hit by gunfire. It all seems so unreal.

Other teachers are coming out of the building to help gather up the students and more gunfire is heard. A scream is heard from over the hill on the field. Students are running everywhere. There is more noise than can be explained. Finally, off in the distance there can be heard sirens.

When the authorities arrive, they find a lone student with a gun in the field over the hill. When students started running in that direction, another student was killed. When the one teacher went to the two students—a very natural reaction—she put herself in harm's way and paid the ultimate price. Altogether in this scenario, four people were killed.

Upon reflection of the aforementioned scenario, there is much that can be learned from that horror. First of all, when teachers are on duty, they need to be stationed in order to monitor as much of the playground as possible. If there is not enough staff to adequately monitor the entire playground, then students need to be restricted to an area that can be well observed.

It is important that teachers carry radios or cell phones in order to communicate with those inside the school in case of an emergency. Students need to know that in a case of an emergency, their responsibility is to be immediately quiet and listen to the teacher. In order for students to react appropriately, they need to have practice. There also needs to be a way to get their attention during the chaos. Even a tiny metal whistle will work, if the students know to react to a whistle. An attitude of triage is important when dealing with crisis. This is the hardest concept to get across to those who have chosen the teaching profession. There are times when you take care of those who are most rather than least likely to survive.

Looking back at this first scenario, it is highly unlikely that the teachers on duty would have deterred the gunman from shooting someone since it was their intent to do so, but the teacher who got killed may have been saved if they dealt with as many students as possible, getting them inside the building instead of running to the two students who were hurt. It is such a natural reaction to help so it is totally understandable that any teacher would want to do that, but who is most important at time like this? The two students or the other 400?

If the students knew that they had to go to the teachers instead of running everywhere, the third student who ran into the field may have not been killed. There are no guarantees in any of this. No crisis situation is exactly like any other, and none are foolproof. For example, a second gunman could have been ready to shoot students as they went into the building, especially if they knew that was the plan. However, having a plan is still critical because it brings some order to the chaos. For example, given the lack of a plan, a student could run off the school premises during such a crisis and go missing, as opposed to going to the designated safe area as according to plan.

How would the authorities properly handle the above scenario once they arrived? They would ensure that the shooter was apprehended. They would check on the well-being of all involved and secure the crime scene. The students would all be brought to their classrooms and accounted for. While efforts are made to calm the students down, no interviewing is done until the proper authorities arrive. Keeping the students in their regular classrooms would help restore some semblance of order and help keep the witnesses accurate. No one would be allowed to change clothes in the case of blood spatters or residue from the crime. This is important to assure full data collection at a crime scene. Students would not be allowed to leave unless under the guidance and direction of the authorities.

Simultaneously, the District Superintendent and Board of Education will be notified. Media and worried parents will flock to the site, so the person in charge of communications would need to get there as fast as possible to direct them to the appropriate holding area. It would be important that no media interviews be held with any students or staff. This, of course, cannot be controlled once the students and staff leave the school, but during the incident, work toward one accurate reporting system. If students were released to parents, there needs to be a system of documenting who each student left with.

Once the shooter and victims are identified, the designated communications authority will inform their families. The communications authority will announce to the media that the incident is over and more regular announcements will be made at a predetermined site. Having the media gather at the predetermined site will not only ensure that the media is provided with important updates, it will also lessen confusion and crowding at the scene of the crime.

There will also be a need to communication with the staff at the other buildings in the district so that they are kept informed and panic is minimized. When there is a concern with one school building, it often sparks panic in other buildings with calls from anxious parents wanting to check on their children and take them out of school. It should therefore be standard procedure to keep all district sites aware of any concerns with another building so that they will know what precautions to take. This recommendation should also be applied to any other form of crisis that will cause community anxiety.

The authorities will then make an announcement that the emergency is over. There will be interviews conducted with students and staff who witnessed the incident. Counselors will be called from other agencies and other buildings to help with immediate sessions with the students and staff. Counseling is not a one-time event; it needs to be ongoing for those involved.

At the end of the day, there needs to be a meeting with the entire staff to discuss all the details and to allow time for reflection before they are sent off. In addition, the documentation needs to be reviewed and edited for accuracy prior to leaving the site. If there were security cameras filming the incident, the footage needs to be downloaded for safe archiving and provided to the authorities as well.

After the authorities are through with the crime scene and approval is given, it is important to clean up the site so that the school can get back to normalcy as soon as possible.

Scenario Two: Hostage Situation

A man walks into the front office and opens up his coat to show he has a gun. He tells everyone in the office area to get into the principal's office. He locks them all in there. He locks the outer doors, checks to be sure no one is hiding anywhere in any of the offices. He puts all the phone lines on hold but using one line, he calls the police and says that they have three hours to get him a car full of gas so he can leave town. If his demands are not met by 11:00 a.m., he is going to bring one person out every half hour and shoot them.

The dispatcher asks a series of questions to try to keep the gunman on the line, but he hangs up. Making sure all the window blinds are drawn on both outside and inside windows, he sits down to wait.

Meanwhile, the rest of the high school is in session, so as with any other school morning, both teachers and students are trying to enter the office, just to find it all locked up with the blinds drawn—which is never the case. One of the lead teachers decides to call the central office to see what might be happening. When the central office has no idea about why the office is still closed, she takes it upon herself to go door to door throughout the entire building to have each teacher lock down their rooms. She reminds them to keep the kids there until there was an all-clear by the authorities as was stated in their crisis manual. She also reminds them to turn their computers on and monitor email. She suggests they continue teaching to keep the students busy, but to not let them out of the rooms for any reason, including bathroom needs.

Soon the teacher notes the quiet arrival of police and firemen. The lead teacher meets the first responders and asks if they need a room to set up as their command post. They agree and do so in the teachers' lounge. The incident command officer attempts to call the front office of the school, but keeps getting a busy signal. He then uses a bull horn outside the front office to try to talk to the hostage taker. The man finally agrees to answer the phone and during the conversation, it is uncovered that he has just escaped from prison where he was incarcerated for murder. His intention is to escape, and he says that while he has no reason to kill anyone, he will if his demands are not met. During this exchange, the incident command officer finds out who is being held in the principal's office. There were two assistant principals, one principal and three secretaries being held. The incident command officer asked to talk to the hostages, but was denied by the gunman who then hung up the phone.

Forty-five minutes pass. The S.W.A.T. (Special Weapons Assault Team) officers are called and they enter the building to ensure that everyone is locked down. At that same time, another team of officers are examining the rooms for any unusual items that could be bombs. They find nothing suspicious, and since the building is very large with wings that have been added over the years, the incident commander decides to escort all classes out of the building using a route that is out of the line of sight for the gunman. Those students closest to the office are kept in a lockdown situation.

The S.W.A.T. team consults with the maintenance supervisor to learn about all entrances and exits to the area where the people are being held hostage. They find an entrance through a large air intake where they can make their way through to the office area. Some of the team members are assigned to that while others are assigned to areas close to the office, both inside and out.

It is one hour and fifteen minutes into the situation, and the gunman has seen no effort to bring the car so he calls out to the incident commander to remind him what he intends to do. The officer asks about how he is feeling and what he thinks he is accomplishing by holding these people hostage and possibly killing them. He keeps his voice very calm, and the gunman responds that he is not going to die in prison and this is his only chance to get away so they had better take him seriously. He cocks the gun so it can be heard over the phone and then hangs up.

By this time, the S.W.A.T. team members are all in place, as many students and teachers as possible have been evacuated, and a flurry of activity is mounting outside from worried parents and the media. A news helicopter is heard overhead. Then, there is another call from the gunman, who was sounding more agitated now. He demands that the car be parked in a certain spot where he can see it, and he says he will take the principal as a hostage to the car and then let him go. The incident commander tells him that the car is on its way and that they intend to meet his demands. He hopes that the gunman will calm down and wait for the car. The gunman hangs up the phone again.

In the meantime, the hostages are trying to get his attention and trying to help him make a better decision. The gunman is not in the mood to hear any of it and tells them to stop talking or he will start killing them sooner. The people in the office remain as quiet as possible, and also try to help one another stay calm. Then they hear an unfamiliar sound and look up to see a black-clad, helmeted, armed man in the large air duct, motioning them to be quiet. They are startled at seeing him there, but the man shows his badge and again warns them silently to not let on that they have seen him.

The gunman is no longer sitting waiting, but pacing back and forth, carefully looking out of the side window, watching for the car. Finally, the car arrives, and he calls the incident commander. His voice is much more agitated than before as he tells everyone to leave the area, to leave the keys on the hood where he could see them, and to leave the front door open on the car. He said once all that is done; he is going to leave with the principal as his hostage, using the emergency exit door.

The hostages hear the exchange and ask him to just leave. He says he cannot take the chance with all the police out there. He needs a shield. He sees that his demands have been met so he opens the door of the office where the hostages were being kept and then brandishing the gun, tells everyone but the principal to get down on the floor with their faces to the floor. They all comply with his demands. The principal reminds the man that he does not have to hurt anyone, but just needs to leave. The gunman grabs the principal and puts the gun to his head, and orders the principal to walk with him. During this exchange, the S.W.A.T. team member in the air duct has his gun drawn and aimed at the gunman.

The principal and the gunman step through the emergency door, and they move toward the car. The gunman immediately sees that the police have moved back but are not gone, so he runs to the car with the principal and then grabs the keys, cocks the gun and aims it at the principal's head. A shot rings out and the gunman goes down. The immediate incident is over.

Scenario Review

This sample hostage situation shows how staff members who know what to do and follow through can help a crisis situation tremendously. The lead teacher, who was likely a member of the safety committee, knew what to do. She did not panic, but brought order to a possible chaotic situation. She helped the first responders. Many of the students would not have even known what was going on when they were escorted from the building. The hostages complied with the gunman's demands and stayed calm, not irritating him further. The incident commander attempted to have a non-deadly outcome of this event, and stayed calm and purposeful throughout the incident. The S.W.A.T. team was assisted by the maintenance supervisor to get into the building to observe and report what was happening in the office. That S.W.A.T. officer was also there to shoot the gunman, if necessary, right there in the office.

After the gunman is taken for medical assistance and the principal is able to get back to his job, he calls the superintendent who was probably at the site. The communications person for the district informs the media to meet at a specified location for an update, taking as many of them away from the school as possible. The parents are told that everything is fine and that school is resuming immediately. There will be a need for psychological support for the hostages and anyone else affected. Everyone will be asked to fully document their experience from their own viewpoint. Most importantly, school would resume.

In this case, we see a potentially disastrous event was foiled due to a thorough crisis plan that was taught to and used by the staff. While this is doubtlessly a traumatic event, those involved will have the knowledge that it was through their good handling of the situation (i.e. following the crisis manual) that a much more catastrophic outcome was averted.

Scenario Three: Hazardous Materials

At noon, a principal is walking around the playground at the elementary building. She is on a side of the building where there are no other people. Many of the students are out for recess on the other side of the building. She notices a strange smell. It makes her cough a bit, so she gets a staff member's attention and asks that all students get back into the building. She uses her cell phone to call the non-emergency number to the police and ask if there is anything to be concerned about. They say they have not heard anything, but they would check into it immediately.

The principal decides that this would be a good drill on how to shelter in place, so she calls for everyone to lockdown and secure their doors and windows. They turn off the ventilation system and wait there until further notice. This staff has done table top drills on sheltering in place so they keep the students working and do not allow anyone out of their rooms. They keep their computers on and monitor their email.

The principal receives a call back from the police chief who says they should shelter in place. She was able to say that they were already tightly locked down. He reports that a methamphetamine house just blew up a few blocks up wind of the school and this was dispersing deadly gas throughout the area. He adds that with the brisk wind, the gas would dissipate quickly but to stay locked down until further notice. The principal emails the staff, explains the situation and asks if any student was showing signs of itching or redness. She herself has a rash on her face, but nowhere else. She goes into the shower and runs water all over herself, fully clothed. She has her secretary continue to check if there were any other people with reactions. At this point, there are none. She calls the superintendent's office to inform the superintendent of the incident.

After totally soaking herself in running water, using no soap, the principal asks for her secretary's coat which she puts on. She then places all her contaminated clothing into a plastic bag. She tells her secretary to call the police chief to tell him that she is going to the hospital and provides him with the name of the designated teacher in charge while she is gone. She then has a staff member take her to the hospital for treatment for what turns out to be very slight burns to her face, and she is released to go back. It turns out that since her face was the only part of her body that was exposed, that was the only body part that was affected, and even then very slightly because she acted quickly. No permanent damage was done. In the meantime, everyone at school was still locked down. After stopping at home for clothing, she goes back to the building in time to get the call from the police, who are collaborating with the hazmat team from the fire department and EMS. She is told that it is all clear and everything has been contained. They can now go about their day as normal.

The principal asks her secretary to draft up a memo relating the incident so it can be copied for the children to take home to their parents. She walks around the building to visiting and checking on every class. She then sits down to document every detail of this crisis. She can take comfort in the knowledge that a potential disaster for the students was avoided, and that a panic was prevented since many of them did not even know of the matter until they got home and heard it on the news.

Reflection on the Scenarios

The purpose of sharing these scenarios is to illustrate the importance of being prepared. While having a plan and following it does not necessarily guarantee that a negative outcome can be averted, it does at least mitigate the negative consequences of a crisis situation.

The post-crisis situation also should not be neglected since it is a time for healing and introspection. After any crisis, it is very important to take time to talk through the event, record any concerns, and any step of the crisis plan that needs to be improved. The lessons learned from a crisis will help build experience in dealing with other forms of possible situations. It is therefore important to reflect on what has happened, how it was dealt with, and how things can be improved.

To recap, the following actions were correctly taken:

- •The administrator verified that there really was a crisis.
- •The administrator or designee calls 911.
- •The superintendent is informed.
- •The administrator activates the school-based crisis team.
- •The faculty controls the students and ensures that directions and procedures are followed.
- •The administrator awaits the all-clear announcement from the incident commander and then announces it to the staff.

The next step is to move into the recovery phase.

Chapter Six

Crisis Recovery

In this chapter, we will discuss and explore:

- What to Do After a Crisis
- Reactions to Violence
- Recovering from Crisis
- Media in a Crisis

What to Do After a Crisis

A crisis situation is now over. There has been an all-clear announcement and it is now time to begin the recovery process. The administrators will feel the strong effects of this post-adrenaline rush. Reactions vary for individuals—they may be very active and excited, or they may be lethargic and very tired. The administrator's supervisor needs to determine if the administrator of the building affected is strong enough at that time to do what is necessary. It makes sense to ensure that our leaders are well enough to lead. If one of the administrators is a victim, then another person needs to step up to get the school through the recovery process. It would be preferable to have these backup leaders chosen ahead of time.

There are different issues to deal with depending on the type of crisis. As in the scenario of the methamphetamine explosion, there was little that anyone could do other than make sure the principal was not seriously hurt and ensure that the students were not affected. They may not have even known about it so it was wise not to get them all upset. It was also a good move for the school to inform the parents so they can answer questions their children may have when they come home. As with any crisis, documentation is necessary for this scenario; however, unlike the usual call for ongoing recovery, it will not be necessary in this situation.

In the hostage situation, there would be much greater need for ongoing counseling, especially for those who were the hostages. The students would need an opportunity to know what went on and to be allowed to share their concerns about it, but large scale student counseling would not be required. The reporting would be very important since this was a crime scene, not just a site that had hazardous gas blow in.

In many crisis situations, it is important that proper support was offered from the school district. Students and staff are not the only people involved in a crisis. Parents become very much involved as well as community members if students and staff were in danger. Questions that might need to be addressed are:

- Is there a need for a meeting or counseling for parents? If so, who is arranging this and when?
- Who will be in charge of that meeting or making arrangements for the counseling assistance?
- If there were injuries or deaths, who will visit those in the hospital or who will attend the funerals?
- There may be requests to have memorials built or hung in schools. It is highly recommended to avoid this. Schools are not meant to be memorials. It is also hard to determine what would be acceptable. Does the school place plaques for students that are killed in a car accident or who die from health reasons? It would get very difficult to continue this through the years. It also gives morbid aura to the facility, taking away from its true focus of teaching and learning.

Reactions to Violence

There will be different reactions to violence. Grief is a very normal reaction and the stages of grief are as follows:

- **Denial**: general feeling of numbness, inconsistent behavior, nightmares, confusion, unfocused preoccupation
- **Fear**: sleeplessness, easily upset or startled, restlessness, false bravado
- **Anger**: sarcastic remarks, anti-social behavior, fighting, irritability
- **Guilt**: often is matched with anger, self-destructive behavior, apologetic, acting out in response to compliments

There are strategies that can be used in the classrooms to help students heal after a crisis. Writing to the one that is hurt or dead is one way for students to help release some of the stress. Creative activities can help students communicate their concerns. Drawing, painting, singing and drama can offer outlets for some students that writing does not provide. Encouraging the class members to help one another empowers some to heal as they assist others to deal with the loss.

Recovering from Crises

There are important factors to consider when recovering from a school crisis. Are there students who are more at risk for post crisis trauma? More intense counseling may need to be provided in these cases. There may also be a need to help staff and families with additional counseling. Outside resources could help with this need.

Post Crisis Reflection

Once the information is gathered from all the areas involved in the crisis, the school should work with the district safety and security committee in making any necessary improvements to the procedures, if such a need was revealed by the crisis.

If the procedures were successful, then the administrators should reflect on why they were effective and how they can be augmented. Everyone learns from this type of discussion and it reinforces the importance of safety knowledge and preparedness. The discussion is also an important morale booster since it brings the entire administrative staff together as a mutual support group during such incidents.

Media in a Crisis

In any crisis that involves police scanners, there will be media involved. Having a developed written statement and an appointed spokesperson to keep the media informed is much more effective since it gets a singular message with the correct information out. The message should include the positive actions that were prepared ahead of the crisis as well as during the crisis. It is important to provide the assigned spokesperson with the information in a timely manner with continuous updates as needed. Depending on the severity of the crisis, the spokesperson may be someone from the law enforcement authorities, instead of the school.

No matter who conveys the information to the media, it needs to be clear, accurate, and avoid any blame or supposition. Facts should be presented in a calm, non-exaggerated manner. The primary concern is to convey the facts without excessive emotion that could distract from the truth.

The media can be of great help in disseminating the information to the community. It is beneficial to help them do their job in informing the public.

Chapter Seven

Debriefing from Crisis,
New Learning and Evaluation

In this chapter, we will discuss and explore:

- Debriefing
- Debriefing Groups
- Ongoing Support
- Reflection on Steps Used in Crisis
- Any Need for Improvement

Debriefing

With all the publicity on school crises over the last few years, a debriefing system is critical—one that allows people to recover at their own pace, and to gather what has been learned through the experience to help improve safety procedures. It is important to bear in mind that there are different purposes for doing debriefing sessions.

The first initial debriefing sessions are likely to be with the law enforcement authorities, who will interview witnesses to the crime.

Debriefing Groups

These groups help the victims and witnesses get through the personal turmoil that follow crisis situations. By being able to share their concerns and hear of others having similar feelings or completely different impressions aids in the healing process.

There is an important need for those involved to have time to deal with the emotional impact of a trauma. A common concern about these sessions is that there will not be enough time for everyone to express their feelings in a debriefing session, but there are strategies that can be used to effectively provide support for large groups of people at one time. The session leaders should preferably be trained in such group debriefing strategies. Sessions can be fairly easily planned and run with some preparation. Having a professionally licensed therapist is ideal, but in many cases there will be none available. Naturally, the more staff members that can be trained in running these sessions, the better off the school is in the event it needs to hold several large debriefing sessions. Details for training resources are provided at the end of this section.

It is suggested that at least two or three people work with a group, if possible. One person acts as a group facilitator and another watches the group's reaction, identifying those that may need more assistance in the future. The third person is a backup. It is most effective to have everyone there for the full session; having the second leader helps in the event that someone leaves midway through the session, this leader can then try to convince them to return to the session. If they refuse, there should be a pre-arranged counselor or another facilitator the person can go to.

There are few guiding principles to use when conducting these debriefing sessions:

- Try to arrange it so that everyone understands that they need to stay in the room for the length of the session. Explain that there will be no notes taken on what each one has said, but that it is a time to share their feelings and observations of the trauma. Everything in that session will remain confidential.
- Ideally, the group size should be less than ten, and last no more than an hour. If the group size is larger, they will need to be broken down into smaller teams and then timed after questions are asked, so that everyone gets a chance to speak.
- In these smaller teams within the larger group, arbitrarily choose someone to go first.
- Have pre-determined questions prepared to use with the group, such as what did you see at 9:00 this morning? Where were you when all of this happened? What did you do when you saw the incident you just described? Is there a personal connection to the victim? How do you feel at this particular moment about this incident? If you feel unsafe, what can be done to make you feel safer now? It would be wise to end with a question like, what have you done in the past that has gotten you through bad situations and can that help you now? Any questions that would aid in the healing process should be posed.
- People are asked the first question and then go clockwise around the group. If one group gets done early within the time allowed, ask them to sit quietly while the rest finish. Do not have them go ahead with a new question. This encourages people to talk and not to rush through the process. It also helps the facilitator handle larger groups.
- Ask them to listen carefully as everyone speaks and not to interrupt anyone.
- Have support materials there, such as tissues and water.
- When the session is over, the facilitators should review how the session went. If there is anyone else they believe needs additional support, they should make the necessary arrangements.

The time frame for doing this initial session should be the same day or the following day after the trauma. It should not be put off—the sooner the better for those who were involved or just concerned about the incident. It would be best to work with the staff first so that they are better prepared to help with the students.

During the debriefing, the facilitators are not there to give answers, but to be supportive and encourage talking among participants. Comments such as "I imagine that was very scary," "Others have reported that, too," and "You are not alone with those thoughts," and "There will be other opportunities to share all of this," could help them feel more comfortable.

The above is just a synopsis of training that professionals can obtain from the *Community Crisis Response Team Manual*, (Second Edition) published by the National Organization for Victim Assistance (NOVA). (1997). Washington, DC: www.try-nova.org.

Discussing the Crisis Manual during debriefing

The debriefing should also include discussions with staff on how the crisis manual strategies worked.

- Reflection on Steps Used in Crisis
- Conversation could be started by asking the following questions: What happened?
- What time did the incident happen?
- Who was involved?
- Was anyone hurt? How?
- Is there any reason for this incident?

To delve into the incident with more specific questions, the following questions could be asked:

- Who reported the emergency and was that conveyed clearly?
- How did the communication with the rest of the required people get accomplished, such as to the superintendent, the full staff and to parents?
- How did the all-clear, emergency-over communication get accomplished? Was it clear and timely?
- Did people handle rumor control?
- How did the triage go with any injured victims?
- How did the relationship with the media go and were they agreeable to an alternative site?
- What areas may need to have further training?
- If evacuation was used, did it go smoothly?
- In the case of evacuation, did the "Go Box" have what was needed?
- If lockdown was used, did it go quickly, and did everyone stay locked down until officials notified everyone?
- Did everyone respect and protect the crime scene?
- Is the school ready to resume or is there a need to relocate to another site?

It is also wise to debrief with the first responders who bring a different perspective and important insight to the discussion. The above questions would help get the conversation started whether the debriefing is with staff or also with the first responders.

At the very least, the staff should take time to talk through the incident from the eyes of the building professionals. What went very well? What could have gone more smoothly? Are the steps that are laid out in the crisis manual effective and usable? Was there anything else that needed to be included to help through an incident such as this again?

Documentation for Improvement Plans

It is important to document and file all paperwork related to the crisis. This is especially critical in the event of any legal action taken.

Once the debriefing has been completed, a comprehensive report that details the effectiveness of the crisis plan and the suggestions for improvement should be completed. If the suggestions are areas that need to be brought to the district safety committee, a plan needs to be made on how and when to get that completed.

If there were suggestions that were reviewed and approved by the district safety committee, these should be added to the procedures for that particular crisis, and the Board of Education's approval should be promptly sought so that these changes can be adopted.

While it is critical that any part of the plan that was not effective be recognized and improved on, it is also just as important to single out what went well. In addition to being a morale booster, positive reinforcement is critical in dispelling any notions that something was not done correctly. By pointing out what was done well, it also sets the standard for what and how things should be done in the event of another crisis. It is therefore important that this list of "do's" is shared with all the administrators at a general meeting.

It may also be good to share that information with the media since it reassures the community about the school's ability to deal with such situations. This is particularly important since the negative events and outcomes were definitely reported. It is therefore vital to balance this picture with what was properly handled.

Finally, personal introspection as a leader is both helpful and healing—a personal reflection on how well you handled the situation will garner much insight into your abilities. What surprised you about your reaction? How did you handle it physiologically? Did you allow people to help you if and when you needed it? It truly is amazing what administrators can do when they are handed such challenges. Undoubtedly, you will be proud of your actions if you were prepared and followed through with your plans.

Chapter Eight

Ongoing Support and Improvement

In this chapter, we will discuss and explore:

- Continuing Vigilance
- Surveillance and Access
- Other Security Concerns
- Refining Crisis Plan
- Final Thoughts

Continuous Vigilance

Prepared districts always refine security plans when new information is received. They need to constantly reevaluate the safety and security of the school and the staff's preparedness to deal with a crisis. All new staff should be fully trained in the safety expectations of the district as soon as possible. School districts also need to make connections with local authorities in drilling and practicing their crisis plans.

Heightened awareness for all staff should be stressed, and that reporting is an expectation and not a choice. There should be constant vigilance. Suspicious people and vehicles should be reported. Suspicious packages should also be reported and handled with caution.

Special attention needs to be applied to the school parameters. What are they and does everyone know where they lie? Who has control of the fences, gates, and is there ongoing review of environmental design as the buildings are renovated? Has the number of accessible entrances been reduced to be controllable? In most elementary schools, this would be the front door only, while in some high crime areas, it may mean having to lock the building entirely with only a buzz-in entrance system.

Surveillance and Access

Secondary schools may need more than one entrance, but it would be wise to have all entrances under surveillance, either with guards or security cameras. Who enters and leaves the school is of major importance, and systems need to be in place to ensure that only those with proper authority are on the site.

Surveillance is important, both by well-trained personnel and effective electronic equipment. There are also other important considerations, such as:

- Are all visitors expected to check in?
- Do staff stop anyone without a visitor pass?
- Is there a regular review of possible open windows or skylights?

- Have all utility areas been locked and secured?
- Do staff on duty know that they are to be vigilant about the parameters and suspicious individuals?
- Are there enough people on duty when students are coming and going at outdoor activities and in the hallways?
- Is it normal procedure to train all new staff in safety and security procedures and expectations?
- Are there sufficient security cameras throughout the district?
- Do personnel know how to read them and watch for unknown people coming and going?
- Does the security camera system have remote access?
- Could the police "see" into the school in the case of an emergency?
- What is the system for delivery notification?
- Are all personnel required to wear identification badges and are they checked?

Another issue is to establish a clear entrance to and exit route from the school site during a crisis situation. In a crisis, the crowds that could descend upon the school site are far greater than we imagine. Frantic parents, for instance, could block responders' access to the site. Could the responders find another way to get onto the site if the traffic were blocked? How has that been designed? Who is in charge of unlocking a gate?

Other Security Concerns to Consider
Procedures:
- Are drivers fully screened?
- Is there control over the building keys when personnel come and go?
- Does the district stay in contact with the significant, related agencies as procedures change?
- Do district level personnel review the procedures every time one is used?
- Have procedures been reviewed with the staff every time they have been revised?

Facilities / Transportation:
- Is there a review of the bus system security?
- Are there security measures in the buses, such as cameras?
- Has access to utility, nutritional services and maintenance areas been secured?
- Have escape drills been held on a routine basis?
- Has access to utility, nutritional services and maintenance areas been secured?
- Have custodians been trained to ensure their understanding of their part to in crisis prevention?

- Are there enough safety supplies in place to handle a crisis in the event that the fire and police are not able enter the building immediately? Such supplies include drinking water, non-perishable food, blankets, battery-operated radio, flashlights, first-aid kit, etc.
- Has the fire alarm system been tested on a regular basis?
- How would the fire system work if no electricity were available?
- Is there a land line that does not need electricity in every building?
- Who is in charge of periodically checking the district web site to ensure there is no unauthorized access to sensitive information?
- Is there a system of utility controls so that telephones, heating and cooling systems, electrical and water systems, under lock and key?

Training:
- Has the staff been offered opportunity to increase their skills in safety and security measures possibly through first aid or CPR?
- Have the nurses in the district had their skills renewed on a regular basis?
- Have custodians been trained on what they are expected to do to help prevent a crisis?
- Have all new classified staff been trained on how to have all food and beverages protected to ensure no contamination?
- Is there a method of ensuring that Building Crisis Plans are renewed on an annual basis or whenever there is a major change in an individual building?

Communication:
- What is the status of the communication systems throughout the district?
- Is there email in place in case that is the only way to communicate?
- What happens to communication if the electricity is not working?
- Who is the spokesperson to outside callers, parents, media?
- How will the information be written to ensure report consistency?
- Where are media to be in case there is a school crisis?
- Has media access been determined ahead of time?
- Does the district have an alternative source for calling parents?
- How will parents know where and when to pick up their children if the school is evacuated?
- Who is in charge and where do they contact the mental health professionals in case of immediate need?
- Who in the district can help? Who in outside agencies have been trained to help in a crisis? Who has their access numbers? Who has the authority to contract with them? Are they always available? Is there a need for a contingency contract?

Refining Crisis Plan

Develop, review, refine, and test the crisis preparedness guidelines. There should be guidelines for both natural disasters and acts of violence. The manual should be updated with any new information on how to handle crisis situations. Particular procedures for handling bombs, bomb threats, hostage situations, kidnappings, chemical and biological terrorism, and related information should be reviewed. An annual staff review about specific roles and responsibilities in respect to the crisis guidelines should be conducted. Identify backup crisis team leaders in case normally assigned leaders are not at the building or are unable to lead. Provide specific grade appropriate security training, crime prevention, and crisis preparedness for the staff. Work hard at not letting your staff lower their guard.

In order to stay current with the equipment, schools districts may need to apply for grants to pay for updating equipment or for brand new items, such as security cameras. To do so, information needs to be sent out to the decision makers, such as the Board of Education and potential sources of funds. The information should include the cost of the equipment and training as well as the purpose and effectiveness of the equipment.

Final Thoughts

The planning for safety and security in schools is not a single event, but rather a continuous process. Once the crisis plan is created, it cannot be assumed that the job has been done—there needs to consistent practice and reminders of the expectations of the district. It will never be over. Constant vigilance is vital to protect our schools. Although school safety has always been a part of the education system, it now occupies a much bigger and more prominent position in the administrator's list of tasks.

Carefully thinking through the possible crisis scenarios is unpleasant and time-consuming for an administrator who already has a substantial list of things to do. However, it is necessary for effective leading during a crisis when staff and students are counting on you. By having a plan, the administrator will be able to provide the much needed guidance through a crisis for the entire school. Being as prepared as possible is not the best thing an administrator can do—it is the only thing they can do in this day and age.

Appendix A

Crisis Planning

Suggested Crisis Manual Inclusions

1. The names and contact details of the Central Office planning team and response team.
2. District and community telephone numbers should be easily accessible.
3. A plan for working with community agencies and planning for recovery after a crisis.
4. The standard individual school crisis plans and required of each school site.
5. Individual building crisis response teams with agreement to serve and training to act.
6. General written expectations for all staff if a crisis occurs.
7. Designee if the Superintendent and/or building principal is not available.
8. Expectations in written form of planning for traumatic events.
9. Specific written follow-up plans.
10. Designation and approval of individual building evacuation sites.
11. List of "go box" items each school would need to take. This box should be ready at all times. Each site will have different needs due to the type of student concerns and location of the evacuation site.
12. Written expectations for following Board approved Crisis Plans.
13. Written expectations and modeling of debriefing of any use of a crisis plan.
14. Design, training and expectation for shelter-in-place strategies. (Often available through the community emergency planning office. But most plans include the following: move people to a pre-determined inside room, close and lock all doors, windows and attempt to seal them tightly, turn off ventilation systems, seal off window air handlers with plastic if available, turn on radio to monitor announcements and for further directions from Emergency Services.)
15. Individual Crisis Intervention Procedures that include as many possible events that occur in that area. The following is a list that could help an organization get started but every agency needs to work through this themselves in order to make it applicable to their area, agency support systems, and building sites. It is not intended to be a complete list since each area may have specific issues to plan for, such as industrial accidents or rural emergency support concerns.
    - Abduction
    - Amber plans
    - Angry/threatening people

- BioTerrorism
- Bus Emergencies including on and off hour concerns
- Chemical warfare and chemical spills
- Deaths in school
- Deaths of people connected to the organization out of school
- Declaration of War
- Earthquakes
- Explosions from fire, plane crashes or intentional acts
- Extreme Heat or Cold Issues
- Facility emergencies, crumbing infrastructure, utility, gas and electric, etc.
- Gunshots or gunmen, inside and outside of a school, which would include students
- Hazmat concerns – Hazardous Materials, including radiological, and nuclear
- Hostage incidents
- Immediate and non-immediate bomb threats
- Intruders
- Suicidal threats both inside and outside of organization
- Terrorism addressed to organization but also to the community
- Threatening or suspicious letters or packages
- Storms including tornadoes, electrical storms, hurricanes, ice and snow

16. A post crisis plan should be created to effectively deal with the hours, days, weeks, and months immediately following the crisis including the anniversary of the event.
17. A plan for media coverage should be included in a crisis manual with possible sample generic letters for immediate communication.
18. Methods of documentation, a communication system, who is responsible should be included.
19. A debriefing checklist should be developed that can be used when each incident occurs.
20. Guidelines for dealing with the public, parents, community members, and the students after a crisis should be created.
21. Working with the support agencies is crucial especially for crises that involve mass care or massive illnesses or even death such as a pandemic.
22. How students can be released to parents or guardians should be determined.

Suggested Sources of Support in Crisis:

FEMA (Excerpts from FEMA web site)

If you have applied for assistance and are contacting FEMA in any manner (telephone, fax, letter, e-mail, visit to Disaster Recovery Center), please present your disaster number and registration number. It is the fastest and most certain way for us to ensure that FEMA is checking your case file, not that of someone else with the same name.

Helpline telephone: (800) 621-3362
Fax: (800) 827-8112
Postal mail: FEMA, PO Box 10055, Hyattsville, Maryland 20782-7055
E-mail: FEMA-Correspondence-Unit@dhs.gov

We cannot tell you prior to your registration or prior to a disaster declaration what disaster assistance, if any, you may be eligible to receive. Some forms of assistance vary by disaster, and some are determined in coordination with the State. In addition, not all counties or parishes in a State are necessarily designated for Individual Assistance in a disaster declaration. In some disasters, additional counties or parishes are designated for Individual Assistance some time after the initial disaster declaration is issued.

If you are not certain whether your county or parish has been designated for Individual Assistance, you may go to http://www.fema.gov/news/disasters.fema, find your State and disaster, then click on the <Designated Counties> box on the far right. Please note that not all counties designated for Public Assistance are designated for Individual Assistance, and that some counties are added to the Individual Assistance list after the initial declaration.

Information is available at the following websites: http://www.fema.gov/pdf/nims/NIMS_basic_introduction_and_overview.pdf, and http://www.fema.gov/plan/mitplanning/faqs.shtm#6. Additionally, you may find information by contacting your State's Emergency Management Agency.

SAFE HAVENS INTERNATIONAL

Safe Havens International is an excellent company that helps organizations begin their safety and security planning. With express permission from Mr. Michael Dorn, Executive Director of Safe Havens International, the following pages in Appendix A have been reproduced from their Free Resources section on their website. Please visit http://www.safehavensinternational.org for more valuable information.

About the Templates

The school safety plan development templates are designed to allow school officials to work closely with local emergency response and community service officials to develop a custom four phase all hazards school safety plan as recommended by the United States Department of Education and Jane's Information Group.

Portions of the templates were tested by several client districts who were recipients of United States Department of Education crisis planning grants. Preliminary tests by these school systems indicate that the templates allow school and local public safety and public service officials to develop a customized four phase plan with about a 75% reduction in the time and effort required. Evaluators also reported that the plan sections they developed using the templates were also of much higher quality.

The full package of school safety plan development templates, which is over 300 pages long, includes:

- A user guide.
- A prevention and mitigation plan development template.
- Response plan templates including master response protocols. Includes integrated flip charts for a variety of categories of employees including lead administrator/crisis response team members, transportation personnel, faculty/staff, custodians and an after hours event flip chart. Each flip chart template is derived from and integrated with the master protocols. Also includes 14 different logs and tracking sheet template.
- A recovery plan template: The United States Department of Education and top recovery experts including Marleen Wong recommend that districts develop a recovery plan and train staff in its use.
- A tactical site survey checklist template
- An exercise package for planning and conducting emergency drills and exercises using a progressive exercise program as recommended by the United States Department of Education, the Federal Emergency Management Agency and Jane's. The exercise package includes more than thirty drills, tabletop exercises and functional exercises complete with messaging slips. The package also includes a variety of exercise design and evaluation forms and checklists. This section will enable a

district with an aggressive exercise program to conduct one drill per school month for three years without repeating a scenario.
- Survey and feedback forms for staff, students, and parents.

Included in this sample are some excerpts from the templates that should provide a strong idea of the comprehensive nature of the templates and their ability to assist a district with the development of a complete crisis plan. There are 15 different sample sections included in this document.

Sample Description

If you are interested in the templates for your district or state, please contact Safe Havens International to discuss pricing and package offers.

Safe Havens International, Inc.
  An IRS approved non-profit School & Community Safety Center
1458 Conestoga Trail
Macon, Georgia, 31220
(404) 557-2068
www.safehavensinternational.org
chris@weakfish.org

The following pages in Appendix A have been reproduced with the kind permission from Mr. Michael Dorn of Safe Havens.

1. Section from the Prevention/Mitigation Plan Template

E.Interior Physical Security and Safety Measures

1. Security cameras provide coverage for key indoor areas at all middle and high schools.
2. All school lockers are kept locked at all times, and students are required to use school locks.
3. The school system has established a procedure for random locker inspections to deter students from keeping weapons in lockers.
4. The school system has established a random metal detection policy. Random metal detection screening is conducted at each middle and high school several times each year.
5. Drug and bomb detection dogs are utilized several times each year to check student lockers and public areas for drugs, firearms, and explosive devices as a deterrent measure.
6. The number of trash containers in use in each school has been minimized. Trash containers are not situated in areas that are out of view. This has been done to reduce the number of potential hiding places for explosive devices and contraband.
7. All schools require that students and school employees wear standardized identification badges with a photograph.
8. All schools have a visitor badge system in place.
9. Each school tests all fire alarm pull stations twice each year to ensure that they function properly.
10. Fire department fire prevention bureau personnel conduct a fire prevention seminar for the staff at each school and facility once annually. Topics include the proper use of fire extinguishers, fire evacuation procedures, common fire code violations in schools, and special concerns for cafeteria personnel.
11. Each school tests the building intrusion alarm system twice each year.
12. The police department crime prevention bureau conducts a crime prevention seminar for staff at each school and facility once annually.
13. Each school has taken steps to properly secure all desktop computers, VCR's and television sets. Security measures include steps to secure computers against theft and unauthorized access.

14. All television sets that are not wall mounted are either bolted to carts or secured using safety straps. District policy prohibits students from being used to move television carts

15. Each school has developed a system to ensure that rooms that are not in use are kept locked.

16. The district has a system in place to ensure that serial numbers are on file for school system property.

17. Valuable school property has been clearly marked to identify it as school property.

18. Each school has established a system to locate, photograph, remove, and report all graffiti to law enforcement in a timely manner.

19. The district uses an internet filtering system. These filtering systems prevent access to sites containing pornography, hate groups, and sites relating to weapon and bomb making materials. The filters are tested through use to make sure they work while not blocking sites needed by students for schoolwork.

20. Each school has developed a system to restrict access to the building during the day by keeping specified doors locked when not in use.

21. Every school has a designated room that is heavily secured. High value equipment is moved to these rooms for storage during extended holidays and summer breaks.

22. The district safety design team has conducted a CPTED (crime prevention through environmental design) and target hardening assessment of each school and facility. Changes have been made as appropriate based on the team's recommendations. Team members have received formal training on CPTED.

23. The district safety design team evaluates all building construction and renovation plans early in the design process and makes recommendations to enhance the level of safety through design features (CPTED and target hardening).

24. Local emergency management, fire service and law enforcement officials have an opportunity to review building construction and renovation plans early in the design process. These officials are afforded an opportunity to make comments on safety and emergency management concerns.

25. The district requires that the architectural firm awarded a building construction or renovation project must have at least one CPTED-trained design team member.

2. Functional Protocol:
Remote Evacuation and Family Reunification

Definition
This type of evacuation is used for any evacuation where students and staff will need to be moved to a remote site for reunification with family members and loved ones.

Alert Signal
Announcement over the public address system "All staff initiate a Code Blue – emergency evacuation in effect at this time, evacuate to site _____located at _____ _____. Please sweep all routes and the site. We will be implementing the Remote Evacuation and Family Reunification Protocol from that location"

Lead administrator Response
1. Notify the central office of your decision to implement the family reunification protocol. Provide a brief description of the incident and specify the staging area so buses can be dispatched to the appropriate location.
2. Request that law enforcement officials dispatch uniformed personnel to the staging area.
3. Activate appropriate crisis teams.
4. Make the announcement by public address system, runners, e-mail or whichever means is most practical "All staff initiate a Code Blue – emergency evacuation in effect at this time, evacuate to site _____ _____located at _____. Please sweep all routes and the site. We will be implementing the Remote Evacuation and Family Reunification Protocol from that location"
5. In certain situations, it may not be practical or safe to order a general evacuation (such as during a hostage situation or if an armed intruder may still be in the area). In such instances, coordinate with public safety officials for law enforcement officials to conduct the evacuation room by room.
6. Designate a staff member to serve as your representative at the family reunification center. Instruct them to take student information from one of the Emergency Evacuation Kits with them.
7. Notify the appropriate crisis team member to serve as your representative at the staging area.

Staff Response

1.Follow non-fire evacuation procedures and guide students to the designated on campus evacuation site. Prepare students for boarding of buses.

2.Ensure that any special needs persons in your area of responsibility are assisted during the evacuation.

3.Once students and other persons from your area of responsibility have boarded a bus, assist the bus driver by taking roll and completing the driver's evacuation roster.

4.Follow the instructions of Family Reunification Staff when you arrive at the Family Reunification Site. You may be asked to assist in staffing the site.

3. Incident Specific Protocol: Bomb Threats/Suspicious Packages

Definition
A bomb threat/suspicious package situation is one that involves the threat of an explosive device that has been placed in, around, or near a facility ,or the detection of a suspicious package that could contain an explosive device.

Alert Signal
Announcement over the public address system "All staff initiate a Code Blue – emergency evacuation in effect at this time, evacuate to site _____located at _____ _____. Please sweep all routes and the site."

Or;
"All staff initiate a sweep in place, please report your status upon completion of the sweep"

Lead Administrator Response
Upon receipt of a bomb threat, the lead administrator should call 911 and request that fire, law enforcement and emergency management personnel respond. If a threat has been received by phone, provide the completed bomb threat checklist (see Appendix A) to the first law enforcement officer to arrive on the scene. Make sure that call tracing procedures have been implemented (keep the phone that the call was received on off the hook so that the call can be traced – if another call comes in afterward this is no longer possible). Consult with responding public safety officials and quickly determine whether it is best under the circumstances to sweep, evacuate and search or to sweep in place. Available information should be evaluated to weigh the potential risks of explosive devices inside the building, explosives devices outside the building (including the possibility of a vehicle bomb), explosives devices placed in or near evacuation routes or sites or other hazards such as persons with firearms who plan to shoot at evacuees. If multiple bomb threats are received over time, be sure to rotate evacuation routes and sites to make it more difficult for someone to pattern your evacuation responses and target evacuees with explosives, firearms or chemical agents.

If the sweep and evacuate option is selected:

1. Notify staff to sweep and evacuate make public address announcement: "All staff initiate a Code Blue – emergency evacuation in effect at this time, evacuate to site _____located at _____ _____. Please sweep all routes and the site." If multiple threats are received over a relatively short time period, be sure to rotate evacuation routes and sites.

2. Have the evacuation route and site swept for suspicious persons, objects (which could contain an explosive device) or other safety hazards prior to the evacuation if appropriate.
3. Have designated staff or public safety officials direct students safely across any streets that must be crossed by evacuees.
4. Remind staff members and students not to utilize cellular or digital phones or portable radios unless a life-threatening emergency exists.
5. Request that uniformed personnel escort staff and students to the evacuation site and remain with them until and unless they are instructed to return to the building.
6. Leave the facility and take the emergency evacuation kit and make responding public safety officials aware of the contents of the kit.
7. Check with staff to see that all evacuees are accounted for. Immediately notify responding public safety officials if any persons are not accounted for.
8. Assist responding public safety officials with the second sweep of the facility.
9. Consult with public safety officials before authorizing evacuees to return to the facility.
10. You may determine that it is appropriate to close the facility for the remainder of the day. If so, begin notification of parents and guardians and implement your emergency release procedures.

If the sweep and remain in place option is selected:

1. Make intercom announcement: "All staff initiate a sweep in place, please report your status upon completion of the sweep."
2. Escort public safety officials through the building to verify that all areas have been swept by staff. Make sure that all areas inside and around the facility have been swept.
3. Assist public safety officials in conducting the second sweep of the facility.
4. If any suspicious packages are noted by staff or public safety officials, make sure that all staff and students are moved away from the item and that it is not disturbed in any way.
5. Consult with public safety officials to see if the facility should be evacuated, if the decision is made to do so, implement the Non-Fire evacuation plan.

Staff Response

Sweep and evacuate procedures:

1. If the sweep and evacuate option is announced, staff should quickly scan their area of responsibility for any packages or items that could contain an explosive device (objects that they do not recognize as normally being present).
2. If no such items are noted, staff should use masking or duct tape to make a slash across the entrance door to the area (/) to indicate to public safety officials they have swept the area and no suspicious items were noticed.
3. If any suspicious items are noted, they should not be disturbed and the staff member should notify the lead administrator or designee upon evacuation from the area.
4. The staff member should then follow the non-fire evacuation protocol. Have students bring their book bags and other hand carried articles with them.
5. Refrain from using cellular or digital telephones or portable radios during these situations unless a life-threatening emergency exists. In some extremely rare instances, radio frequency energy can trigger an explosive device to detonate. Explain to students that any electronic communication devices that are observed in use will be seized. Explain to the students that the use of such devices can pose a safety hazard.

Sweep and remain in place procedures:

1. Staff members should scan their area of responsibility for any packages or items that could contain an explosive device (objects that they do not recognize as normally being present).
2. If no such items are noted, staff should make a slash with masking or duct tape across the entrance door to the area (/) to indicate to public safety officials that they have swept the area and no suspicious items were noted. Take a roll to account for all persons in your area of responsibility in case evacuation is ordered at a later time.
3. If any suspicious items are noted, they should not be disturbed. The staff member should then direct all people in the area to follow them to the lead administrator's office and inform the lead administrator or designee of his or her observations.
4. Follow the lead administrator's instructions.

4. Lead Administrator/Crisis Response Team Member: Remote Evacuation and Family Reunification Protocol

Definition

This type of evacuation is used for any situation in which students and staff need to be moved to a remote site for reunification with family members and loved ones.

Alert Signal

Announce over the public address system "All staff initiate a Code Blue – emergency evacuation in effect at this time, evacuate to site _____located at ____ _____. Please sweep all routes and the site. We will be implementing the Remote Evacuation and Family Reunification Protocol from that location"

Lead administrator Response

1. Notify the central office of your decision to implement the family reunification protocol. Provide a brief description of the incident and specify the staging area so that buses can be dispatched to the appropriate location.
2. Request that law enforcement officials dispatch uniformed personnel to the staging area.
3. Activate appropriate crisis teams.
4. Make the announcement by public address system, runners, e-mail or whichever means is most practical "All staff initiate a Code Blue – emergency evacuation in effect at this time, evacuate to site _____ _____located at _____. Please sweep all routes and the site. We will be implementing the Remote Evacuation and Family Reunification Protocol from that location"
5. In certain situations, it may not be practical or safe to order a general evacuation (such as during a hostage situation or if an armed intruder may still be in the area). In such instances, coordinate with public safety officials for law enforcement personnel to conduct the evacuation room by room.
6. Designate a staff member to serve as your representative at the family reunification center. Instruct him or her to take along student information from one of the Emergency Evacuation Kits.
7. Notify the appropriate crisis team member to serve as your representative at the staging area.

5. Transportation Flip Chart:
Remote Evacuation and Family Reunification Protocol

Definition
This type of evacuation is used for any evacuation where students and staff will need to be moved to a remote site for reunification with family members and loved ones. Transportation personnel need to be familiar with two very different scenarios for this protocol, relocation from an affected school, and relocation from an affected bus.

Alert Signal
Notification by dispatcher or in person notification by route supervisor

Driver Response
For an incident involving your bus:
1. Follow non-fire evacuation procedures and guide students to an appropriate evacuation site. Prepare students to board another bus.
2. Ensure that any special needs persons are assisted during the evacuation.
3. Once students have boarded a bus, assist the bus driver by taking roll and completing the driver's evacuation roster.
4. Follow the instructions of Family Reunification Staff when you arrive at the Family Reunification Site. You may be asked to assist in staffing the site.

Route Supervisor Response
1. Notify dispatch and the central office of your decision to implement the family reunification protocol. Provide a brief description of the incident and specify the staging area so a bus can be dispatched to the appropriate location.
2. Request that law enforcement officials dispatch uniformed personnel to the staging area.
3. If you must stay at the scene, designate a staff member to serve as your representative at the family reunification center.

When one or more schools are affected by a crisis
Driver Response
1. When you are notified that your assistance is needed for implementation of the family reunification plan, make sure that you have copies of student family reunification rosters.
2. Follow directions provided by route supervisors and public safety officials as to the best approach to the affected school or its evacuation area.

3. Try to calm students as they board the bus.
4. Once loaded, proceed safely to the family reunification site. Understand that evacuees may be traumatized by events and may be in an excited and emotionally distraught state.
5. Have a staff member fill out the student transport roster. If no staff member is present, ask a student to perform this task and note the name of the student who completed this task on the form.
6. Do not stop the bus or open the door to allow evacuees to meet family members.
7. When you arrive at the family reunification site, follow the instructions of public safety and crisis team personnel. Provide the roster(s) to the Crisis team member that meets your bus.
8. Return for the next relay if you are needed and repeat the process until the evacuation is complete.
9. Your bus may or may not be escorted by law enforcement depending on the available resources and the nature of the crisis.
10. Keep all radio traffic to a minimum.

Supervisor Response
1. Advise all drivers to keep the radio clear except for important transmissions until the last transport is completed.
2. Work with administrators at the affected site, crisis response team members and public safety officials to set up an efficient relay system. Designate a staging area near the school so buses can be staged there if too many buses arrive at the evacuation area at one time for loading.
3. Maintain a log of the status of all involved buses to help you keep track of available resources.
4. If buses from another school system or mass transit buses are sent to assist, coordinate with their supervisors and personnel. Attempt to establish a means of radio communications with their personnel. You may be able to provide a spare radio to a representative of their organization.
5. Brief your supervisor as appropriate.

6. Faculty/Staff Flip Chart:
Remote Evacuation and Family Reunification Protocol

Definition
This type of evacuation is used for any evacuation where students and staff will need to be moved to a remote site for reunification with family members and loved ones.

Alert Signal
Announcement over the public address system "All staff initiate a Code Blue – emergency evacuation in effect at this time, evacuate to site _____located at ____ _____. Please sweep all routes and the site. We will be implementing the Remote Evacuation and Family Reunification Protocol from that location"

Teacher Response
1. Follow non-fire evacuation procedures and guide students to the designated on campus evacuation site. Prepare students for boarding of buses.
2. Ensure that any special needs persons in your area of responsibility are assisted during the evacuation.
3. Once students and other persons from your area of responsibility have boarded a bus, assist the bus driver by taking roll and completing the driver's evacuation roster.
4. Follow the instructions of Family Reunification Staff when you arrive at the Family Reunification Site. You may be asked to assist in staffing the site.

7. Custodian's Flip Chart:
Remote Evacuation and Family Reunification Protocol

Definition
This type of evacuation is used for any evacuation where students and staff will need to be moved to a remote site for reunification with family members and loved ones.

Alert Signal
Announcement over the public address system "All staff initiate a Code Blue – emergency evacuation in effect at this time, evacuate to site _____located at _____ _____. Please sweep all routes and the site. We will be implementing the Remote Evacuation and Family Reunification Protocol from that location"

Custodial Response
1. Follow non-fire evacuation procedures and guide students to the designated on campus evacuation site. Prepare students for boarding of buses.
2. Ensure that any special needs persons in your area of responsibility are assisted during the evacuation.
3. Report to the lead administrator/staff member/Crisis Response Team member and provide assistance as needed. Assistance may include:
4. Aiding Crisis Response Team members in sweeping all or part of the facility to ensure that all occupants are evacuated.
5. Aiding Crisis Response Team members in securing the facility.
6. Once you are advised to evacuate to the family reunification site and students and other persons from your area of responsibility have boarded a bus, assist the bus driver by taking roll and completing the driver's evacuation roster.
7. Follow the instructions of Family Reunification Staff when you arrive at the Family Reunification Site. You may be asked to assist in staffing the site.

8. After Hours Activities Flip Chart:
Remote Evacuation and Family Reunification Protocol

Definition

This type of evacuation is used for any evacuation where students and staff will need to be moved to a remote site for reunification with family members and loved ones.

Alert Signal

Announcement over the public address system, bullhorn, or other means "We are activating our Family Reunification protocol. Students, staff and visitors will be transported to _____ to be reunited with their loved ones.

We ask for your assistance and cooperation. Buses will pick us up at _____

All staff initiate a Code Blue – emergency evacuation in effect at this time, evacuate to site _____located at _____. Please sweep all routes and the site. We will be implementing the Remote Evacuation and Family Reunification Protocol from that location"

Lead Staff Member Response

1. Coordinate with public safety officials and/or Crisis Response Team members when deciding which site to use. Unlike a daytime emergency, another school or athletic stadium may be appropriate.

2. Notify _____ of your decision to implement the family reunification protocol and request that the Crisis Response Team be activated and sent to the selected site. Request that Crisis Response Team members have someone dispatched to the selected site with master keys. Provide a brief description of the incident and specify the staging area so buses can be dispatched to the appropriate location.

3. Request that law enforcement officials dispatch uniformed personnel to the staging area.

4. Make the announcement by public address system, runners, e-mail or by the most practical means available to inform visitors, staff and students. It may be best to wait until the Crisis Response Team and buses have had time to travel to the affected site and the family reunification site before making the announcement and moving to the staging area.

5. In certain situations, it may not be practical or safe to order a general evacuation (such as during a hostage situation or if an armed intruder may still be in the area). In such instances, coordinate with public safety officials for law enforcement officials to conduct the evacuation room by room.

6. Designate a Crisis Response Team member or other staff member to serve as your representative at the family reunification center. Instruct

them to take student information from one of the Emergency Evacuation Kits with them.

7. Notify the appropriate crisis team member to serve as your representative at the staging area.

9. Response Plan Templates: Incident Tracking Sheet

Use official command post time. Please use ink.

Location of Incident:

Type of incident: **BOMB THREAT/NON-FIRE EVACUATION**

Sheet initiated by:

Date:

1st Shift
Relieved by:
Time:

2nd Shift
Relieved by:
Time:

3rd Shift
Relieved by:
Time

ACTION	ORGANIZATION	STATUS	NOTES	REPORTED BY
Notify appropriate public safety (police, fire)				
Select an evacuation route and site				
Activate appropriate crisis teams				
Send designated staff member(s) to sweep the evacuation route and site				
Announce evacuation				
Sweep the facility for students and adults, assist special needs persons				
Ensure that the emergency evacuation kits are removed from the building				
Evacuate according to non-fire evacuation protocol				
Report to the first responding public safety official				
Report to the evacuation site				
Decide whether to implement the family reunification protocol				
Implement the media protocol				
Once at the site, develop a written list of all evacuees				
Confiscate any electronic communications devices that are prohibited by policy				

Time and date log closed out:

Name of person closing log:

Incident Tracking Sheet received by:

Date received:

Witnessed by:

Date:

10. Recovery Plan Templates: Death Notification Protocol

1. Verify the name of the deceased with the police.
2. Contact the school administrative office and/or the attendance office and request that all correspondence concerning the student and/or staff member be stopped. Delete the student's name from all school mailing lists.
3. Do not go alone. Contact another death notification team member to accompany you.
4. Have grief resources available such as fact sheets about grief, to give to the family (brochures, hotline numbers, web sites, etc.)
5. Talk about reactions to the death with your team member(s) before the notification to enable you to better focus on the family when you arrive.
6. Provide the notification in person. **Do not call**. If the Family Reunification Center has been established provide, the notification in the Counseling Area Only. Pick a quiet, private area away from the other counseling rooms.
7. Introduce yourself and the other team member, present credentials and ask to come in. Remember, only one member should talk.
8. Sit down, ask the other party to sit down, and be sure you have the nearest next of kin (do not notify siblings before notifying parents or spouse). Never notify a child. Do not use a child as a translator.
9. Ensure that the correct family/survivors are in the room. Use the victim's name... "Are you the parents of _____?"
10. Look at the family member/survivor in the eye and speak face to face. Inform them of the death in a simple fashion and direct manner with warmth and compassion. Do not use expressions like "expired," "passed away," or "we've lost _____." Remember to add your condolence. Adding your condolence is very important because it expresses feelings rather than facts, and invites them to express their own.
11. Continue to use the words "dead" or "died" through on-going conversation. Continue to use the victim's name, avoid using the terms "body" or "the deceased."

School District Death Notification Team

The following is a list of the _____ School District Death Notification Team.

NAME	SCHOOL NAME	CONTACT NUMBER	TRAINING DATE

Tips for Delivering Death Notification

1. Do not use clichés.
2. When a child is killed and one parent is at home, notify that parent and then offer to take them to notify the other parent.
3. Never speak to the media without the family's permission.
4. Do not leave survivors alone.
5. Call and follow up the next day with a visit.
6. Ask the family how and when they would like personal possessions delivered. Do not assume that clothing should be washed. Inventory items and pack in a box. Do not deliver personal items in a plastic bag or trash bag.
7. Do not discount feelings, theirs or yours. Intense reactions are normal. Expect fight, flight, freezing, or other forms of regression. If someone goes into shock have them lie down, elevate their feet, keep them warm, monitor breathing and pulse, and call for medical assistance.
8. Know exactly how to access immediate medical or mental health care should family members experience a crisis reaction that is beyond your response capability.
9. Do not blame the victim in any way for what happened, even though he/she may have been fully or partially at fault.
10. Join the survivors in their grief without being overwhelmed by it.
11. Answer all questions honestly (requires knowing the facts before you go). Do not give more detail than is asked for, but be honest in your answers.
12. Offer to make calls, arrange for child care, and call clergy, relatives and employers. Provide them with a list of the calls you make as they will have probably have difficulty remembering what you have told them.
13. Debrief your own personal reactions with caring and qualified disaster mental health personnel.

11. Section from Comprehensive Tactical Site Survey Template

Hallways and Main Areas:

Yes	No	Can doors be quickly secured during a lockdown?
Yes	No	Is visibility through classroom windows unimpeded?
Yes	No	Clear directional signage?
Yes	No	Are classrooms marked by number and not by teacher's name?
Yes	No	Are the numbers located on the wall next to the classroom and are they unobstructed?
Yes	No	Are they raised numbers and fastened in a permanent fashion?
Yes	No	Are they visible when the door is open?
Yes	No	Are all unused lockers secured?
Yes	No	Is someone assigned to conduct a "morning sweep" of the building interior to identify anything out of the ordinary or potentially dangerous?
Yes	No	Are wall electrical panels locked?
Yes	No	Is a fire extinguisher located on each hallway in a visible area and checked regularly for operability?
Yes	No	Are all the fire pull stations functioning properly?
Yes	No	Does each hallway have a minimum of 6-feet of clearance from one side to the other?
Yes	No	Are exit doors clear of obstructions and easy to operate in an emergency?
Yes	No	Are all hallways clear of coat racks?
Yes	No	Are tornado evacuation areas away from skylights and windows?
Yes	No	Are pay phones blocked from receiving incoming phone calls?
Yes	No	Are pay phones located within view of the office staff or monitored by video surveillance?
Yes	No	Do motion detectors cover all entrances and main hallways?
Yes	No	Do classroom doors open inward?
Yes	No	Do classroom doors swing "in the clear?"
Yes	No	Are all ceiling tiles are in place?
Yes	No	Is the interior directional signage for specific locations adequate?
Yes	No	Are all bookrooms, teacher's lounges, custodial closets, and electrical rooms are always secured/locked?
Yes	No	Are the fire exit lights functioning properly?
Yes	No	Is there a functioning emergency lighting system in the hallway?
Yes	No	Are all chemicals and cleaning supplies put up and out of the way?
Yes	No	Are interior fire doors magnetic and do they contain windows?
Yes	No	To these doors remain unobstructed?
Yes	No	Does the magnetic system appear to be functioning properly?
Yes	No	If surveillance cameras are present, do they appear to cover areas near bathrooms and building entrances adequately?
Yes	No	If shaded, bubble protectors are used, are they cleaned routinely?
Yes	No	Do all hanging plants, displays, and/or wall-mounted objects have closed eye-hooks and can they swing freely 45 degrees?
Yes	No	Are fluorescent light bulbs, lenses, and covers securely fastened?
Yes	No	Are large windows located in the hallways made of safety glass or do they have shatter-resistant film on them?
Yes	No	Are display cases or aquariums protected against overturning or sliding off tables?
Yes	No	Are valuable, fragile art objects or trophies protected against tipping over, breaking glass or sliding off shelves or pedestals?
Yes	No	It is very dangerous to chain doors in occupied buildings. There should be no chains on the doors of the facility. Is this the case?
Yes	No	Are lockers locked with school locks?

Yes	No	Is graffiti documented by camera or video and promptly removed?
Yes	No	Are there any indicators on ceiling tiles that they are used as hiding places for contraband?
Yes	No	Are the paper towel and toilet tissue holders see-through plastic?
Yes	No	Are the paper towel and toilet tissue holders locked?
Yes	No	Are all soap dispensers or other items on the wall in current use?
Yes	No	Do the bathrooms have hallway doors?
Yes	No	Are the hallway doors lockable?
Yes	No	Are trashcans plastic?
Yes	No	Are trashcans open-topped?
Yes	No	Do you conduct frequent checks of your trashcans that can result in the discovery of contraband under the plastic liner in the can?
Yes	No	Do interior hallway fire doors remain unobstructed during the day?

12. Sample Items from the Exercise Package

Sample drill scenario:

Emergency bus evacuation drills
All staff and students should participate in at least one emergency bus evacuation drill each year. This is necessary as students who ordinarily do not ride the bus may need to ride a bus during a field trip or emergency evacuation. Students who regularly ride the bus should participate in additional drills. Many school districts conduct additional drills for special needs buses since evacuation procedures are more complex.

Sample tabletop exercise scenario:

Rape of a teacher in her classroom after hours
It is 7:40 P.M. and your crisis response team has been activated due to a reported sexual assault of a teacher at your school. Upon arrival at the school, you meet with other team members in the cafeteria and are briefed on the incident by the principal and a detective. You are told that a teacher regained consciousness in her portable classroom building (or classroom if your school does not have portable units) after being beaten unconscious with a fire extinguisher. Her clothing had been ripped off and a medical exam confirms that she has been raped. She is unable to recall what happened, but it appears that an intruder entered her room and attacked her with the fire extinguisher before raping her. The teacher is in stable condition at the hospital and the incident is under investigation.

Sample functional exercise scenario:

Airplane crash
At 7:35 am a 707 aircraft takes off from the local Airport during a thunderstorm. As it is climbing, it encounters a wind shear condition at an altitude of 250 feet. Within seconds, the plane slams into a commercial/residential area three quarters of a mile south of the airport and five miles from an elementary school and a middle school. Upon impact, the plane is torn apart and leaking jet fuel ignites. Dozens of stores, warehouses, and single-family homes are destroyed over a three-block area. There are numerous injuries and fatalities among passengers and people on the ground. A fire has been reported at the elementary school. Fire/rescue units from the city and from the Airport respond to the scene. They encounter a situation that will require their full resources and capabilities. Additional fire/rescue and police units are requested to report to the elementary school, as well as the fire mobile command post. On-lookers and media personnel have arrived and are standing too close to the hazardous area as well as interfering with incident response operations. Parents are calling the school district offices and the schools.

Questions

1. Who is in charge at the school level?
2. How will you coordinate the services of many agencies and jurisdictions that will respond?
3. How will you deal with the parents?
4. How will you deal with the media?
5. How will you handle school buses that are en route?
6. How will the victims be treated and transported to hospitals?
7. Where will the family reunification site be set up?
8. Who and what agencies will disseminate official information to the public?

Sample generic and scenario specific messages:

MESSAGING SLIPS FOR HAZMAT FUNCTIONAL EXERCISE
LEAD ADMINISTRATOR/PRINCIPAL: You have just had a heart attack, please get up and walk out
LEAD MENTAL HEALTH OFFICIAL: Several people claiming to be mental health professionals have shown up. They want to know where to report.
TEACHER: A student is having an asthma attack.
SECRETARY: You receive a high volume of calls from parents wanting information.
ANNOUNCEMENT TO ALL PLAYERS: 3 students at Town A Elementary School are ill with watery eyes and shortness of breath.
DISTRICT LEAD ADMINISTRATOR: You are notified that several teachers are experiencing severe panic attacks. They have abandoned the children under their care and left the building.
SCHOOL NURSE: You receive a report that the crisis team leader has passed out.
PUBLIC INFORMATION OFFICER: 5 international media outlets are requesting press kits about the situation.
PRINCIPAL: Residents in the area are demanding information about the situation.
DISTRICT REPRESENTATIVE: Several city and county officials are demanding a briefing on this event.
ANNOUNCEMENT TO ALL PLAYERS: Due to the high call volume, the phone system has shut down.
ANNOUNCEMENT TO ALL PLAYERS: Several parents are trying to get into the school to pick up their children. They are beating on the doors demanding to retrieve their children.
PRINCIPAL: The school secretary has lost control and is yelling, "Everyone is going to die!"
PUBLIC INFORMATION OFFICER: Please go to the front of the room and deliver a press briefing.
PRINCIPAL: The county manager would like a briefing from you. Please leave the room for 10 minutes.
ANNOUNCEMENT TO ALL PLAYERS: The Incident Commander is requesting someone to come to the command post. Please have this person get up and leave the room for 10 minutes.
LEAD ADMINISTRATOR: 5 students have become ill and will need to be transported to the hospital.
ANNOUNCEMENT TO ALL PLAYERS: Who is in charge at this point? Quietly write your answer down and give it to the facilitator, who will assess the answers and share findings with the group.

13. Sample Questions for Participants to Use in Functional Exercises

District Staff
Notification/Coordination
With what outside agencies are you coordinating?
How are you communicating (equipment, processes, etc.)?
Who will need to be notified at this point?
Operations
How will schools and school offices be evacuated?
Where will operations be conducted (Command Post)?
What staff will be needed to support this incident?
What is the threat level at this point?
Response
Who is in charge?
How will response efforts be coordinated?
Recovery
How is family reunification coordinated?
What other recovery activities will occur?
Who will coordinate recovery activities?
Public Information
How are parents notified?
What information should be released at this point? Why?

14. Sample Exercise Checklists: Emergency Programs

Indicate the status of each program to determine those in need of practice:

Program	New?	Updated?	Practiced?	Used?
Emergency Operations Plan				
Recovery Plan				
Family Reunification Protocols				
Resource List				
Emergency Public Information				
Emergency Alert System				
Emergency Transportation				
Parent Notification Procedures				
Mutual Aid Agreements				
Coordination				
Emergency Operations Staff				
Volunteer Staff				
Emergency Operations Center				
Communications				
Other:				
Other:				
Other:				

Appendix B

Federal Communication

UNITED STATES DEPARTMENT OF EDUCATION

THE DEPUTY SECRETARY

October 6, 2004

Dear Colleague:

The recent terrorist attack against a school in Beslan, Russia, was obviously a shocking incident worldwide. Understandably, the horror of this attack may have created significant anxiety in our own country among parents, students, faculty, staff and other community members, particularly in light of the graphic details that many of us saw in the news. Today, I am writing to share information with you regarding some lessons learned from the Beslan school incident in an effort to better understand how it happened and apply lessons that might be used to protect U.S. schools.

For your background, the U.S. Department of Education (ED) works closely with the Department of Homeland Security (DHS) and the Federal Bureau of Investigation (FBI), and we have teamed together with them on this important school safety issue. DHS and the FBI have recently analyzed the Beslan situation and shared their analysis with state and local law enforcement officials in your community, which is why I wanted to share that information with you as well. Again, they have done this in an effort to use the information to safeguard American schools and our students. The analysis was done proactively; it was not sent out due to any specific information indicating that there is a terrorist threat to any schools or universities in the United States.

You should also know that DHS and the FBI, as a part of their analysis, have encouraged local law enforcement officials to maintain contact and open lines of communication with local school administrators such as you and to ask personnel to report any suspicious activities.

While I am aware that many of our nation's schools have been developing comprehensive crisis plans and that ED widely disseminated informational material in August called "Practical Information on Crisis Planning," I also believe the following information will be useful as you update your plans. The FBI-DHS analysis described some specific protective measures that I would also like to share with you, many of which would be applicable to a variety of potential emergency situations, including natural disasters.

Short-term protective measures include reviewing procedures to safeguard school facilities and students and others within them. Those recommended in the DHS-FBI bulletin include:

- Review all school emergency and crisis management plans. Helpful guidance can be found at www.ed.gov/emergencyplan/.
- Raise awareness among local law enforcement officers and school officials by conducting exercises relating to school emergency and crisis management plans.
- Raise awareness among school officials and students by conducting awareness training relating to the school environment that includes awareness of signs of terrorism.
- Raise community awareness of any potential threats as well as vulnerabilities.
- Prepare the school staff to act in a crisis situation.
- Consider a closed-campus approach to limit visitors.
- Consider a single entry point for all attendees, staff and visitors.
- Focus patrols by law enforcement officers on and around school grounds.
- Ensure that school officials will always be able to contact school buses.
- Ensure that emergency communications from and to schools are working.
- Download the Red Cross brochure, *Terrorism: Preparing for the Unexpected*, at http://www.redcross.org/services/disaster/keepsafe/terrorism.pdf and provide a copy to students, staff and faculty.
- Report any suspicious activity to law enforcement authorities.

Long-term protective measures should include physical enhancements to school buildings. Among the measures schools should consider are the following:

- Install secure locks for all external and internal doors and windows.
- Install window and external door protections with quick-release capability.
- Consider establishing a safe area (or safe areas) within the school for assembly and shelter during emergencies.
- Apply protective coating on windows in facilities that face traffic. That and other helpful information on school facilities can be found at www.edfacilities.org/.

In the analysis they provided to local law enforcement officials, DHS and the FBI have also outlined activities to watch for that may suggest potential unwelcome surveillance of educational facilities. These indicators alone may in fact reflect legitimate activity not related to terrorism. Multiple indicators, however, could suggest a heightened terrorist or criminal threat. They are:

- Unusual interest in security, entry points, and access controls or barriers such as fences or walls;
- Interest in obtaining site plans for schools, bus routes, attendance lists and other information about a school, its employees or students;
- Unusual behavior such as staring at or quickly looking away from personnel or vehicles entering or leaving designated facilities or parking areas;
- Observation of security reaction drills or procedures;
- Increase in anonymous telephone or e-mail threats to facilities in conjunction with suspected surveillance incidents;
- Foot surveillance involving individuals working together;
- Mobile surveillance using bicycles, scooters, motorcycles, cars, trucks, sport utility vehicles, limousines, boats or small aircraft;
- Prolonged static surveillance using people disguised as panhandlers, shoe shiners, food, newspaper or flower vendors, or street sweepers not previously seen in the area;
- Discreet use of still cameras, video recorders, or note-taking at non-tourist locations;
- Use of multiple sets of clothing and identification or the use of sketching materials (paper, pencils, etc.);
- Questioning of security or facility personnel; and
- Unexplained presence of unauthorized persons in places where they should not be.

It is my hope that you carefully review this information and work with your security staff, local law enforcement, first responders and emergency preparedness personnel to ensure that these protective measures are included in your School Crisis Plan. I encourage you to visit ED's Web site on crisis planning, www.ed.gov/emergencyplan/, where additional information about key elements of a crisis plan can be found.

To help with questions that parents, students, faculty and other community members may ask, we have developed a series of the most frequently asked questions regarding the issue of responding to a crisis in general. (See attached.) I have also included a list of available resources if you would like more information on a variety of topics, from crisis planning to how to talk to children about these types of incidents. In addition, I am enclosing information about various ED grant programs concerning school safety that may be of interest.

In closing, I want to assure you that we are working very closely with DHS, the FBI, the Department of Justice, the Department of Health and Human Services and the Secret Service to ensure that our schools and our children in them remain safe. And, again, the information recently provided by DHS and the FBI to state and local law enforcement was not generated by any threats received by U.S. educational institutions -- it was a routine communication reflecting their analysis of the Beslan incident.

Thank you for your attention to this matter, and please feel free to call the U.S. Department of Education's Office of Safe and Drug-Free Schools at (202) 260-3954 for more information or if you have any questions. We look forward to hearing from you.

Sincerely,
/S/
Eugene W. Hickok
Deputy Secretary
Attachments

Resources Available for Schools

Information, Guides and Reports
Emergency Plan Web Site

The Department of Education's (ED) Office of Safe and Drug-Free Schools' Emergency Plan Web site www.ed.gov/emergencyplan provides a one-stop site for information to help plan for, mitigate, respond to and recover from any emergency (natural disasters, violent incidents, terrorist acts and the like). The site provides access to ED materials, such as *Practical Information on Crisis Planning,* and links to additional emergency planning resources of government agencies, nongovernmental organizations, health-care provider resources, mental health resources, and state and local resources.

Practical Information on Crisis Planning:
A Guide for Schools and Communities

This binder provides schools and communities with basic guidelines and useful ideas on how to develop and refine their emergency response and crisis management plans for each phase of crisis planning: mitigation and prevention, preparedness, response and recovery. This information is available at www.ed.gov/emergencyplan/.

Infrastructure Protection:
National Clearinghouse for Educational Facilities

This Web-based clearinghouse at www.edfacilities.org provides information on school safety issues, such as how to design buildings to prevent or mitigate possible terrorist attacks and violence.

Bomb Threat Assessment Guide:
ED and Bureau of Alcohol, Tobacco and Firearms

The *Step-by-Step Guide for Bomb Threats* can assist school districts, administrators and emergency responders in planning an effective bomb threat response protocol in schools. A CD/ROM interactive planning tool provides schools with a 15-step guide. In 2003, a copy of the CD/ROM was distributed to every school district in the country. It is still available at www.ed.gov/emergencyplan/.

Campus Public Safety Guide

The Department of Homeland Security's Office of Domestic Preparedness published a series titled *Campus Public Safety: Weapons of Mass Destruction and Terrorism Protective Measures* in April 2003. This document describes affirmative steps colleges and universities can take to prevent, deter or effectively respond to an attack by weapons of mass destruction. It is available at www.ed.gov/emergencyplan/.

Safe Schools Initiative: ED and the U.S. Secret Service

The 2002 *Safe Schools Initiative Guide and Final Report* provides guidelines for managing threatening situations and offers ways to create a safe school environment. It is available at www.ed.gov/emergencyplan/.

Information Specifically for Children

A Web site with age-appropriate information for children on disasters is at www.fema.gov/kids/. In addition, the Department of Homeland Security is working to expand its citizen preparedness "Ready" campaign by getting children involved in preparing for crises. The Web site is planned to be launched later this year.

Information Dealing With Trauma

The National Child Traumatic Stress Network Web site http://www.nctsnet.org/nccts/nav.do?pid=ctr_tool contains the following links to tools and materials that can be used by schools both for school planning purposes and as handouts to parents and caregivers:

The link to "Presentation Tools" http://www.nctsnet.org/nccts/nav.do?pid=ctr_tool_present allows one to view and download slide presentations on selected topics related to child trauma and traumatic stress, including statistics on the prevalence of child trauma, current interventions to reduce the impact of child traumatic stress, and an overview of the National Child Traumatic Stress Network.

The "Educational Materials" link http://www.nctsnet.org/nccts/nav.do?pid=ctr_tool_educ includes tip sheets for parents, caregivers, and teachers on current topics, as well as basic information on child traumatic stress for different audiences.

Grants Available From the U.S. Department of Education
Emergency Response and Crisis Management Discretionary Grants

Emergency Response and Crisis Management grants provide funds to local educational agencies to improve and strengthen their emergency response and crisis management plans. This year, ED is obligating 105 awards for a total of $28 million. ED anticipates conducting another competition in the area of crisis planning in fiscal year 2005. We anticipate that a notice regarding the competition will be issued in a few months.

The Safe Schools-Healthy Students Initiative Grants

These grants provide students, schools and communities with federal funding to implement a comprehensive plan of activities, programs and services focusing on promoting healthy childhood development and preventing violence and alcohol and drug abuse. In fiscal year 2004, ED contributed a total of $95 million for grants supporting this initiative. Other federal departments also contributed funds. We anticipate additional funding for this initiative in fiscal year 2005.

Questions and Answers

Q. Why is the Department of Education sending this information? Is there an imminent threat to America's schools?
A. The FBI and DHS are currently unaware of any specific, credible information indicating a terrorist threat to public or private schools, universities or colleges in the United States. The FBI and DHS have told us that there is no imminent threat to U.S. schools and that the group that conducted the operation in Russia has never attacked or threatened to attack U.S. interests. However, in an abundance of caution, the Department of Education and our federal law enforcement partners are providing state and local law enforcement officials and educators with an analysis of some of the important lessons learned about the recent incident in Beslan, Russia.

Q. Who else have federal officials contacted regarding the Beslan incident?
A. The DHS and FBI recently sent an analysis of the Beslan incident to their constituents in the law enforcement field. The Department of Education (ED) is distributing information to our constituents in the education community. Among those to whom ED is sending the information are: school police and school security personnel; school resource officers; emergency response and crisis management grantees; chief state school officers; members of boards of education; organizations representing principals; institutions of higher education; and various groups representing non-public schools. Our intent is to inform all appropriate school-related constituencies, all types of schools, whether public or non-public, and institutions of higher education.

Q. How should those informed respond to the bulletin?
A. School districts, in partnership with local law enforcement officials and first responders, should review their crisis plan, ensure that it is up to date, practice their plan, and make modifications as needed.

Q. What should we tell parents and students?
A. We believe you need to be truthful and open. You need to tell students that there are no imminent threats to U.S. schools but that there is a continued need to be prepared to deal with a wide range of crises that can occur in schools and communities.

Q. Are there any resources available at the federal level to help us with our crisis planning?
A. Yes, there are numerous Web pages, booklets, manuals, clearinghouses, etc. available to help you. A summary of resources is found as an attachment to this document.

Q. What about financial resources? Does ED have any financial resources to assist school districts?

A. ED anticipates conducting another competition in the area of crisis planning in fiscal year 2005. We anticipate that a notice regarding the competition will be issued in a few months.

The following was provided by FEMA and is a public document:

NIMS Basic FEMA 501-1

Introduction and Overview

I. Purpose: This document provides introductory NIMS information and an overview of the topics covered by the *NIMS Basic* document set.

II. Scope: NIMS provides a consistent nationwide template to enable Federal, State, local, and tribal governments and private-sector and nongovernmental organizations to work together effectively and efficiently to prepare for, prevent, respond to, and recover from domestic incidents, regardless of cause, size, or complexity, including acts of catastrophic terrorism.

A. **Background** – While most incidents are generally handled on a daily basis by a single jurisdiction at the local level, there are important instances in which successful domestic incident management operations depend on the involvement of multiple jurisdictions, functional agencies, and emergency responder disciplines. These instances require effective and efficient coordination across this broad spectrum of organizations and activities. Since the September 11, 2001, attacks on the World Trade Center and the Pentagon, much has been done to improve prevention, preparedness, response, recovery, and mitigation capabilities and coordination processes across the country. A comprehensive national approach to incident management, applicable at all jurisdictional levels and across functional disciplines, would:

- Further improve the effectiveness of emergency response providers and incident management organizations across a full spectrum of potential incidents and hazard scenarios.
- Also improve coordination and cooperation between public and private entities in a variety of domestic incident management activities.

B. **HSPD-5**:
- Issued by the President on February 28, 2003.
- Directs the Secretary of Homeland Security to develop and administer NIMS.
- Requires all Federal departments and agencies to:
  - Adopt the NIMS.
  - Use it in their individual domestic incident management and

           emergency prevention, preparedness, response, recovery, and mitigation programs and activities.
- Use it in support of all actions taken to assist State, local, or tribal entities.
- Make adoption of the NIMS by State and local organizations a condition for Federal preparedness assistance (through grants, contracts, and other activities) beginning in FY 2005.

- Requires the Secretary of Homeland Security to develop a NRP that integrates Federal government domestic prevention, preparedness, response, and recovery plans into a single, all-disciplines, all-hazards plan.

C. NRP – The NRP uses the comprehensive framework provided by the NIMS to provide the structure and mechanisms for:

- National-level policy and operational direction for Federal support to State, local, and tribal incident managers.
- Exercising direct Federal authorities and responsibilities as appropriate under the law.

D. NIMS Compliance – Jurisdictional compliance with certain aspects of the NIMS will be possible in the short term, such as adopting the basic tenets of the ICS identified in the NIMS document. Other aspects of the NIMS such as data and communications systems interoperability, however, will require additional development and refinement to enable compliance at a future date.

E. NIMS Basic – This series of documents is extracted from FEMA 501, *National Incident Management System* and contains a bullet item reformat of text extracted from the original document. Each document is one chapter or appendix from the NIMS, and uses the same wording to allow easy comparison of the documents. Always refer to the NIMS in case of questions or conflicting information. *NIMS Basic* is organized with the purpose, scope, and definitions at the front of the document. The *Process* section follows and contains the main body of the document. References and supersedure information are at the end.

III. Table of Contents:

IV. Definitions:

emergency response providers – The term as defined in the Homeland Security Act of 2002, Section 2(6) includes the following Federal, State, local, and related personnel, agencies, and authorities. (6 U.S.C. 101(6))

- Emergency public safety.
- Law enforcement.
- Emergency response.
- Emergency medical (including hospital emergency facilities).

FY – Fiscal Year

HSPD-5 – Homeland Security Presidential Directive - 5, *Management of Domestic Incidents*

ICS – Incident Command System

incidents – This can include:

- Acts of terrorism.
- Wildland and urban fires.
- Floods.
- Hazardous materials spill.
- Nuclear accidents.
- Aircraft accidents.
- Earthquakes.
- Hurricanes.
- Tornadoes.
- Typhoons.
- War-related disasters.

- etc.

local government – Defined in the Homeland Security Act of 2002, Section 2(10) as:

- County.
- Municipality.
- City.
- Town.
- Township.
- Local public authority.
- School district
- Special district.
- Intrastate district.
- Council of governments (regardless of whether the council of governments is incorporated as a nonprofit corporation under State law).
- Regional or interstate government entity.
- Agency or instrumentality of a local government.
- An Indian tribe or authorized tribal organization.
- In Alaska, a Native village or Alaska Regional Native Corporation.
- A rural community.
- Unincorporated town or village.
- Other public entity. (6 U.S.C. 101(10))

NIC – NIMS Integration Center

NIMS – FEMA 501, *National Incident Management System*

NRP – FEMA 510, *National Response Plan*

State – Defined in the Homeland Security Act of 2002 as:

- Any State of the United States.
- The District of Columbia.
- The Commonwealth of Puerto Rico.
- The Virgin Islands.
- Guam.
- American Samoa.
- The Commonwealth of the Northern Mariana Islands.
- Any possession of the United States. (6 U.S.C. 101(14))

V. Process: The NIMS uses a systems approach to integrate the best of existing processes and methods into a unified national framework for incident management. This framework forms the basis for interoperability and compatibility that will, in turn, enable a diverse set of public and private organizations to conduct well-integrated and effective incident management operations.

1. Core Set – NIMS enables effective, efficient, and collaborative incident management at all levels through a core set of:
   • Concepts.
   • Doctrine.
   • Principles.
   • Procedures.
   • Organizational processes.
   • Terminology.
   • Technologies.
   • Standards requirements applicable to a broad community of NIMS users.
       a) *HSPD-5 HSPD-5 identifies the core set as:*
          • The ICS.
          • Multiagency coordination systems.
          • Unified command.
          • Training.
          • Identification and management of resources, including systems for classifying types of resources.
          • Qualifications and certification.
          • Collection, tracking, and reporting of incident information and incident resources.
2. NIMS The NIMS document:
   • Establishes the basic elements of the NIMS and provides mechanisms for the further development and refinement of supporting national standards, guidelines, protocols, systems, and technologies.
   • Is not an operational incident management or resource allocation plan.
   • Builds on the foundation provided by existing incident management and emergency response systems used by jurisdictions and functional disciplines at all levels.
   • Integrates best practices that have proven effective over the years into a comprehensive framework for use by incident management organizations in an all-hazards context (terrorist attacks, natural disasters, and other emergencies) nationwide.
   • Sets in motion the mechanisms necessary to leverage new technologies and adopt new approaches that will enable continuous refinement of the NIMS over time.
   • Was developed through a collaborative, intergovernmental partnership with significant input from the incident management functional disciplines, the private sector, and nongovernmental organizations.
   • Provides for interoperability and compatibility among Federal, State, and local capabilities.

B. Concepts and Principles – The NIMS is based on an appropriate balance of flexibility and standardization to provide the framework for interoperability and compatibility.

1. Flexibility The NIMS provides a consistent, flexible, and adjustable national framework within which government and private entities at all levels can work together to manage domestic incidents, regardless of their cause, size, location, or complexity. This flexibility applies across all phases of incident management: prevention, preparedness, response, recovery, and mitigation.

2. Standardization The NIMS provides a set of standardized organizational structures such as the ICS, multiagency coordination systems, and public information systems, as well as requirements for processes, procedures, and systems designed to improve interoperability among jurisdictions and disciplines in various areas, including:
   - Training.
   - Resource management.
   - Personnel qualification and certification.
   - Equipment certification.
   - Communications and information management.
   - Technology support.
   - Continuous system improvement.

C. Overview – The NIMS integrates existing best practices into a consistent, nationwide approach to domestic incident management that is applicable at all jurisdictional levels and across functional disciplines in an all-hazards context.

Six major components make up this systems approach. Each is addressed in a separate *NIMS Basic* document.

Of these components, the concepts and practices for Command and Management and Preparedness are the most fully developed, reflecting their regular use by many jurisdictional levels and agencies responsible for incident management across the country.
- FEMA 501-2, NIMS Basic - Command and Management
- FEMA 501-3, NIMS Basic - Preparedness

The following documents introduce many concepts and requirements that are also integral to the NIMS but that will require further collaborative development and refinement over time.
- FEMA 501-4, NIMS Basic - Resource Management
- FEMA 501-5, NIMS Basic - Communications and Information Management
- FEMA 501-6, NIMS Basic - Supporting Technologies

> • FEMA 501-7, NIMS Basic - Ongoing Management and Maintenance

D. NIMS Components

The following synopsis of each major component of the NIMS describes how these components work together as a system to provide the national framework for preparing for, preventing, responding to, and recovering from domestic incidents, regardless of cause, size, or complexity. A more detailed discussion of each component is included in the NIMS and the respective *NIMS Basic* document.

1. Command and Management

    NIMS standard incident command structures are based on the following three key organizational systems.

    a) *ICS*

    The ICS defines the operating characteristics, interactive management components, and structure of incident management and emergency response organizations engaged throughout the life cycle of an incident;

    b) *Multiagency Coordination Systems*

    These define the operating characteristics, interactive management components, and organizational structure of supporting incident management entities engaged at the Federal, State, local, tribal, and regional levels through mutual-aid agreements and other assistance arrangements.

    c) *Public Information Systems*

    These refer to processes, procedures, and systems for communicating timely and accurate information to the public during crisis or emergency situations.

2. Preparedness Effective incident management begins with a host of preparedness activities conducted on a "steady-state" basis, well in advance of any potential incident. Preparedness involves an integrated combination of:

    • Planning.
    • Training.
    • Exercises.
    • Personnel qualification and certification standards.
    • Equipment acquisition and certification standards.
    • Publication management processes and activities.

    a) *Planning*

        • Describes how personnel, equipment, and other resources are used to support incident management and emergency response activities.

- Provides mechanisms and systems in support of a full spectrum of incident management requirements for:
    - Setting priorities.
    - Integrating multiple entities and functions.
    - Ensuring that communications and other systems are available and integrated.

b) *Training Includes standard courses on:*

- Multiagency incident command and management, organizational structure, and operational procedures.
- Discipline-specific and agency-specific incident management courses.
- The integration and use of supporting technologies.

c) *Exercises*

Incident management organizations and personnel must participate in realistic exercises, including multidisciplinary, multijurisdictional, and multi-sector interaction, to improve integration and interoperability and optimize resource utilization during incident operations.

d) *Personnel Qualification and Certification*

Qualification and certification activities are undertaken to identify and publish national-level standards and measure performance against these standards to ensure that incident management and emergency responder personnel are appropriately qualified and officially certified to perform NIMS related functions.

e) *Equipment Acquisition and Certification*

Incident management organizations and emergency responders at all levels rely on various types of equipment to perform mission essential tasks. The acquisition of equipment that will perform to certain standards, including the capability to be interoperable with similar equipment used by other jurisdictions is a critical component of operational preparedness.

f) *Mutual Aid*

Mutual-aid agreements are the means for one jurisdiction to provide resources, facilities, services, and other required support to another jurisdiction during an incident. Each jurisdiction should be party to a mutual-aid agreement with appropriate jurisdictions from which they expect to receive or to which they expect to provide assistance during an incident.

g) *Publications Management*

Publications management refers to:

- Forms and forms standardization.
- Developing publication materials.
- Administering publications, including:
    - Establishing naming and numbering conventions.
    - Managing the publication and promulgation of documents.
    - Exercising control over sensitive documents.
- Revising publications when necessary.

3. Resource Management

The NIMS defines standardized mechanisms and establishes requirements for processes to describe, inventory, mobilize, dispatch, track, and recover resources over the life cycle of an incident.

4. Communications and Information Management

The NIMS identifies the requirement for a standardized framework at all levels of incident management for:

- Communications.
- Information management (collection, analysis, and dissemination).
- Information-sharing.

a) *Incident Management Communications*

Incident management organizations must ensure that effective, interoperable communications processes, procedures, and systems exist to support a wide variety of incident management activities across agencies and jurisdictions.

b) *Information Management*

Information management processes, procedures, and systems help ensure that information, including communications and data, flows efficiently

through a commonly accepted architecture supporting numerous agencies and jurisdictions responsible for managing or directing domestic
incidents, those impacted by the incident, and those
contributing resources to the incident management
effort. Effective information management:
- Enhances incident management and response.
- Helps ensure that those involved in crisis decision-
making are better informed.

5. Supporting Technologies
Technology and technological systems provide supporting
capabilities essential to implementing and continuously refining
the NIMS. These include:
- Voice and data communications systems.
- Information management systems such as record keeping and
resource tracking.
- Data display systems.
- Specialized technologies that facilitate ongoing operations
and incident management activities in situations that call for
unique technology-based capabilities.

6. Ongoing Management and Maintenance
This component establishes an activity to provide strategic direction
for and oversight of the NIMS, supporting both routine review and
the continuous refinement of the system and its components over
the long term.

E. Additional Publications
The Secretary of Homeland Security, through the NIC discussed in FEMA
501-7, *NIMS Basic - Ongoing Management and Maintenance*, will:
- Publish separately the standards, guidelines, and compliance protocols
for determining whether a Federal, State, local, or tribal entity has
adopted the aspects of the NIMS that are in place by October 1, 2004.
- On an ongoing basis, publish additional standards, guidelines, and
compliance protocols for the aspects of the NIMS not yet fully
developed.

F. Appendices
The appendices to the NIMS provide additional system details regarding the
ICS and resource typing. These are also available as:
- FEMA 501-8, *NIMS Basic – The Incident Command System.*
- FEMA 501-9, *NIMS Basic – Resource Typing System.*

VI. References:

FEMA 501, *National Incident Management System*

FEMA 501-1, *NIMS Basic - Introduction and Overview*

FEMA 501-2, *NIMS Basic - Command and Management*

FEMA 501-3, *NIMS Basic - Preparedness*

FEMA 501-4, *NIMS Basic - Resource Management*

FEMA 501-5, *NIMS Basic - Communications and Information Management*

FEMA 501-6, *NIMS Basic - Supporting Technologies*

FEMA 501-7, *NIMS Basic - Ongoing Management and Maintenance*

FEMA 501-8, *NIMS Basic – The Incident Command System*

FEMA 501-9, *NIMS Basic – Resource Typing System*

FEMA 510, *National Response Plan* Homeland Security Act of 2002

HSPD-5, *Management of Domestic Incidents*

VII. Supersedure: Original

Appendix C

Suggested Sources for Further Information

Bureau of Alcohol, Tobacco and Firearms
Department of the Treasury
Room 2209 Pennsylvania Ave, N.W.
Washington, D.C. 20226
Bomb and Physical Security Planning
202/566-7395

FBI, Threat Assessment
Critical Incident Response Group
National Center for Assessment of Violent Crime
FBI Agency
Quantico, Virginia 22135
Web site: http://www.fbi.gov/publications/school/school2.pdf

National Organization for Victims Assistance
NOVA, 510 King Street, Suite 424, Alexandria, VA 22314
Phone: (703) 535-NOVA
Fax: (703) 535-5500
http://www.trynova.org/

United States Department of Education
Safe and Drug-Free Schools Program
400 Maryland Avenue, SW
Washington, DC 20202-6123
Phone: 202/260-3954
Fax: 202/260-7767
Web site: www.ed.gov/offices/OESE/SDFS

United States Secret Service
National Threat Assessment Center
950 H Street NW, Suite 9100
Washington, DC 20223
Phone: 202/406-5470
Fax: 202/406-6180\Web site: www.secretservice.gov/mtac

Youth Suicide National Center
1825 Eye Street, N.W., Suite 400
Washington, D.C. 20006
202/429-2016

Printed in the United States
69455LVS00005BB/3-8